FIVE-MOUNTAIN MORNING

COVER PAINTING BY GYANNE SMITH
COVER DESIGN BY LINDSAY HADLEY

The author thanks the following for their kind permission to re-print material included in this book:

Pp. 23 and 45: The description of UPI's "Elvis notebook" and "A Whole Slew of Kittens" are copyrighted and used with permission of *The Courier-Journal*, Louisville, Ky.
P. 39: A verse from "Kisses Sweeter Than Wine," words and music by Pete Seeger, Huddie Ledbetter, Fred Hellerman, Ronnie Gilbert, and Lee Hays, is reprinted with permission of TRO-Folkways Music Publishers, Inc.
P. 54: An excerpt from "A Tale" from *The Blue Estuaries* by Louise Bogan (copyright © 1968 by Louise Bogan; copyright renewed 1996 by Ruth Limmer) is reprinted with permission of Farrar, Straus & Giroux, LLC.
Pp. 83 and 86: Excerpts from "In Transit" by W.H. Auden are reprinted with permission of Random House, Inc.
P. 109: A verse from "Seeing Off the Mountain Monk Ch'u, Returning to Japan," by the T'ang dynasty poet Chia Tao is reprinted with permission of the translator, Michael O'Connor.
P. 176: The linoleum block print, "Spaceship #1," is reproduced with permission of the artist, Colin Bridges.

Art credits: The sketch "Gail Beverly" on Page 103 is by Vilko Gecan and was a gift from the artist to the author. The sketch by Easy Romine, Page viii, is in the author's possession. The engraving of a Roman triumph on Page 154 is from *Pinnock's Improved Edition of Dr. [Oliver] Goldsmith's Abridgement of the History of Rome*, Thomas Cowperthwaite, Philadelphia, 1846.

"Five-Mountain Morning," by William Bridges. ISBN 1-58939-791-6.

Manufactured in the United States of America.

Five-Mountain Morning

A memoir by
William Bridges

BY THE AUTHOR OF 'UNDER THE HEAVEN TREE'

ALSO BY WILLIAM BRIDGES

Poetry

Common Places

Weedpatch or Jericho?

The Arafura Sea

The Perfect Country of Words

Eye

*The Landscape Deeper In:
Selected Poems, 1974-2004*

Other

*Dear Viola: Reporting, Writing and Editing
for the Student Journalist*

*Under the Heaven Tree:
An Indiana Childhood*

A Dedication

When I began writing this memoir, after an earlier childhood one, there was a certain amount of good-humored comment from my four sons. "I guess this is the one in which *we* finally appear," Karl said. David and Mike weighed in with a thought or two, and lawyers were mentioned. But Colin added, "Say anything you want. I probably deserve it." I began to realize there was an expectation of some sort.

There is a good reason, though, why they (and their mother) appear somewhat tangentially in these pages—fathers and husbands have no business trying to characterize seriously their loved ones. Life is hazardous enough—they must tell their own stories.

This is not to say that I haven't thought a lot about them, or that our relationships are not *fraught*—that wonderful word. But I've followed the example of my own father, who loved his children without analyzing them. We seemed to be a source of happy amazement to him, and he rarely tried to advise us. I, for one, appreciated this and think it may be one of the best gifts fathers can give their children. Others feel differently—I'm thinking of one father who wrote long, wisdom-filled letters to his son at college. The boy did not appear to have been damaged by this, but then I don't know how seriously he read the letters, between classes and the fraternity party.

On the other hand, sons are expected to write about their fathers and about the *fraughtness* of the relationship. Sir Osbert Sitwell, the British writer, spent much of five volumes doing so, and it's delightful reading. The fascination and eccentricity of the old man's character seem to be all that kept Sitwell from killing him.

In an old notebook, I find a quotation from Mike, age 6: "Mom, do you have to have one of those polka-dot handkerchiefs to run away from home?" Your parental units are glad none of you ever had handkerchiefs.

Contents

The author, as sketched by a traveling carnival artist, Easy
Romine, at the Johnson County, Indiana, Fair, about 1954.

PREFACE

Five-Mountain Morning

O n a clear day, you can see forever," says the Broadway show tune. It's a pleasant thought, even an inspiring one, but I don't want to see that far, at least not yet. A five-mountain morning will do just fine, thank you.

When I lived in Taipei for 13 months in 1993-94, it was in a jewel box of a top-floor apartment, with polished wood everywhere and a view out over the city to the surrounding hills. From the roof garden a flight up, one could see the city's famed mountain, Yangmingshan. I filled the rooms with blossoms from the Taipei Flower Market next door.

It was a perfect love nest of an apartment, which could finally fulfill its purpose when Karen, my wife, came for a month's visit. We checked the view each morning, but Taipei is one of the world's most polluted cities, and sometimes there was nothing to see. At other times, there was just the dull silhouette of the first ring of hills—maybe a shadowy range or two beyond. But occasionally, on one of those crystal days that Taipei calls "typhoon weather," a shout would go up, "It's a five-mountain morning!" and the hills would be visible all the way to the farthest skyline. (This is how we counted, anyway; we didn't do a topographical survey.)

In considering this book and an earlier childhood memoir, I think I've had an astonishing number of five-mountain mornings. Taipei itself was one of them, metaphorically, for I woke

1

up and saw things that had been veiled from me until then. When I came home, most people were content with a quick description of life abroad, but my friend Kathy Carlson asked the pertinent question: "What did you learn about yourself?" The answer: plenty! Vision is the most powerful metaphor I know; I was constantly seeing my life in new ways through the lens of Taipei.

Metaphors can be pressed too far, but the mountains came to mind when I began writing a second, adult memoir. Such sequels are tricky; the charm of childhood is gone, and the writer faces the twin perils of boring readers with details of a fairly ordinary life and career, or of simply telling stories. Mine *has* been an ordinary life, in outline anyway—several years abroad, 25 years as a newsman, and another 25 as a teacher. Some travels, a family, and friends. I have tried not to bore, or to overdo the anecdotes. But you, reader, will have to judge whether you are seeing a mountain now and then, or whether the writer is simply fogged in.

The childhood memoir, *Under the Heaven Tree*, took matters to about the age of 23, when I was drafted into the Army, with a few quick looks beyond. This new account begins with the Army.

When *Heaven Tree* appeared, one reader—a boyhood friend—wrote, "I hope this wasn't all true." His comment puzzled me, and still does. I had tried to get all the checkable facts right, but truth? There is no guarantee that any of us can see that clearly. It's enough usually to see to the second or third ring of hills, with an occasional blesséd five-mountain morning.

But if there should turn out to be, in some matchless dawn, a six- or even a seven-mountain morning, oh yes!

CHAPTER 1

A Dog-Faced Soldier

A sergeant herded 20 of us—college boys, others—into a room at Jefferson Barracks in St. Louis. It was 1957. We were the ones who didn't have draft deferments or who, like me, had stupidly let them lapse. In the room were two long tables, each divided by low partitions into cubicles. Atop the table in each cubicle was a chair.

"Siddown!" barked the sergeant and walked out. Someone, a born leader of men, climbed onto a table and sat in a chair. The rest of us followed. We were hunched there on the table top, facing forward like passengers in a bus, when the sergeant returned.

"All right, you guys," he said, enunciating carefully. "Get down off the tables. Put your chairs on the floor, *facing* the tables. *Then* sit down in the chairs, and I'll give you your intelligence test."

I could almost end the story of my two-year Army career right there. It's amazing that an army, any army, ever wins a battle. It's amazing it even finds its way to the mess hall for breakfast. When I read about the efficiency of our military— shock and awe, etc.—I believe in the technology, because ordinary soldiers without electronic brains would screw everything up. I say this as a former member of an elite unit, the 3rd Infantry "Rock of the Marne" Division, sent to Germany in the spring of 1958 on "gyroscope" or rotation duty. Our predecessors had caused a lot of trouble by drinking, raping, pillaging, and generally sabotaging German-American relations. We had been hand-picked for our intelligence and higher education. The Army soon found that we drank, raped, and pillaged like anybody else; we just used better grammar while doing it. We also sang:

> *I'm just a dog-faced soldier*
> *with a rifle on my shoulder,*
> *and I eat raw meat for breakfast every day.*

On the Marne, I imagine, it had been "eat a Hun for breakfast."

After basic training in the pine woods of Ft. Benning, Ga., the new division, including our public information office, boarded the *Gen. Alexander Patch* in Savannah harbor and sailed away to Germany. As editor of the division newspaper, the *Marne Rock,* I had colored tags that allowed me to go almost anywhere on the ship, including the radio room for the paper's daily skeletonized budget of world news. This taught me a lesson for later life as a journalist: the guts of almost any news story can be told in one sentence.

Arriving in Bremerhaven, the information staff talked its way ashore and spent a long and increasingly blurry afternoon in various *bierstuben.* "Gegrundet 1546" said a sign in one. No bar in Vincennes, Indiana, was older than 1940, and German beer was definitely not Miller Lite or Champagne Velvet, Indiana's pallid brew. I have a picture taken the next day as the troops finally debarked from the *Patch.* The real soldiers are lined up holding flags, but we information specialists are all over the place, striding importantly with clipboards, writing in notebooks, focusing cameras, having the time of our lives.

At Bremerhaven we boarded trains for our post in Würzburg, Bavaria, where we would be the first, and expendable, line of defense should the Soviet Army decide to pour through the Fulda Gap. Headquarters Company lived in Leighton Barracks, an old German army *kaserne* on a hill overlooking the city. On another hill was a massive medieval fortress, the Festung, visible for miles in all directions. Taking the new troops in hand, an information specialist who was heading home after two years told us, "There's a big fortress on a hill on the other side of town. It's called the Festung, and you ought to visit it. I just found out last week it was there."

The story of my year and a half in Würzburg has something to do with the Army, but more to do with beer, friendship, love, travel, and the discovery of cultures older than that of the Hoosier Midwest. The Army part revolved around our boss, Maj. Arch Roberts, an ex-advertising man from Denver. Roberts had been known for such things as having soldiers re-enlist while parachuting. After two years with us, he became information officer for Maj. Gen. Edwin Walker, whose "Pro Blue" troop-education program was criticized as right wing. Walker lost his command, and Roberts later got in trouble for making an unauthorized speech to the Daughters of the American Revolution, in which he suggested that Los Angeles Mayor Sam Yorty had a Communist background.

But the major kept clear of politics while with the 3rd Division, although he was gung-ho in other ways. For months before going to Germany, our office plastered the German media with news of the "combat-ready Marne Division" and its nuclear potential. The German Socialist press made great hay with this, so there was some immediate fence-mending to do.

Then someone decided it would be a service if the *Marne Rock* published the locations of all 3rd Division units. Soldiers would be able to see where their friends were. We were printing at *Stars and Stripes* in Darmstadt, where an informer ratted to Army intelligence; we spent a long night clipping maps from thousands of newspapers. This led the major to transfer our printing to the Würzburg *Main Post*, a German newspaper.

I had my own reasons for the change, since my assistant, Ted Wetzler, had been throwing up in my hat during our weekly flight by small plane to Darmstadt. At the *Main Post,* a gifted and patient printer, Horst Piewak, put the paper together for us each week and became the first of many German friends.

Life under Major Roberts could be a trial. He had trouble remembering our names and would call for us by our functions. I was "Newspaper!" which was easy. But who was "Files!"? And who, for heaven's sake, was "Scissors!"? On a memorable day, one of us passed through his office and spotted a scribbled note: "A-Stan—3rd Infantry to go instead of 8th." We

5

were invading Afghanistan? The office split between the single soldiers, who were intrigued by the idea, and the married ones with apartments downtown, who told us to shut up and return to reality. Then came the major's bellow: "Maps!" We looked at each other. "Bring me one that shows Central Asia!" It turned out that the division drill team was to march alongside a Soviet team in Kabul on Afghan independence day. We were never allowed to write a news release—stories of Cold War cooperation were a no-no, and I am probably breaking security to reveal it now. But perhaps Army intelligence no longer knows where I live.

Except when he was chewing me out for dirty fingernails, Major Roberts and I got along reasonably well, but I learned a life lesson: if I could survive the Army under the major, no other job or boss would ever daunt me. Another lesson came from Sgt. Calvin Murray, our office NCO. During a rainy maneuver, he sent us to steal a ditching shovel from the captain's quarters. Soon the captain appeared, raging, demanding his shovel. (It was leaning against the tent wall.) Sergeant Murray smiled, was affable and understanding, smiled some more, could certainly see why the captain was concerned, would look into the matter promptly. The captain's rage gradually spent itself and he left muttering, without his shovel. The Murray Démarche is a tactic I have used often.

Military life, except for lifers, is mindless, galling, and devoid of any redeeming social value. One soon gets tired of singing:

> I wouldn't give a bean
> to be a fancy-pants Marine,
> I want to be a dog-faced soldier like I am.

Boredom leads young men and women to do things they would eschew in real life, like cutting off the bootlaces of Ralph, the company idiot, by a quarter of an inch a day to see how long it will take him to notice. Ralph, being incapable of most duties, had been assigned to fire the sunset cannon. It was trained in our direction, and we were happy that he had no live ammunition. In the real Army units—the infantry companies in places like Bamberg and Schweinfurt—it was rumored that serious soldiering took place. But in headquarters company, things were looser. My friend and sports editor, Max Nichols, was walking with Major Roberts when a recruit threw a snappy salute. "Why can't you salute like that, Nichols?" the major growled. "Because I'm only on temporary duty from civilian life, sir," Max replied.

Despite the Cold War, it was a peaceful time to be a soldier in Germany. Almost too peaceful. When President Eisenhower sent troops into Lebanon, I asked the major to let me go where the action was. He said no. I went around him to 7th Army, which also said no; I was needed on the *Marne Rock.* Ted Wetzler went instead and wrote funny letters back about the boredom and how Special Services had spent its entire budget on 6,000 pairs of football shoes. Another *Rock* staffer, Bill Manly, and I learned German together by walking around Würzburg, babbling, " Das ist ein Baum," "Das ist eine Strassenbahn," "Ein Bier, bitte." One day we set out to rent a boat on the Main River. "Bitte, können wir ihr Boot zerreisen?" we asked the concessionaire. "You want to do *what* with my boat?" he cried in German. We had gotten the past tense of "rend," and had asked, "Please, can we rip your boat apart?"

All of us got away from the Army as much as possible, to drink wine at the Festung or beer at the Café Blasius, around the corner from the *Main Post,* where it was always afternoon. We visited Horst and his wife Maria, sampled the city's many good restaurants, enjoyed its annual Kiliani Fest and Mozart Week, and made friends with as many interesting Würzburgers as possible. In a way we were carrying out the Army's plan to improve German-American relations, although not quite in the way intended.

I did my part by falling in love with a German girl who worked at the post library. She was beautiful, intelligent, spoke excellent English, and had a lovely name, Silke von Borstal. After a few dates, I proposed to her over lunch at the Walfisch Café on the Main River, and she did me the kindness of thinking it over for a day before saying, gently, no. I think the proposal surprised me almost as much as it did her. For the first time I thought deeply about what it might mean to go through life with someone, and about what it had meant to my parents and other couples I knew.

(While writing this, I asked Bill Manly if he remembered Silke. "Who could forget?" he replied. "What a beauty. I didn't realize that while I was mooning over her from afar in the post library, you not only had gotten as far as knowing her full name, but actually had proposed." He added that he believes at least one other GI in our unit also had offered "to take her away from all this," and had also been turned down—gently.)

When not in love or exploring Würzburg, I took furloughs to Munich and Rome, bicycled through the Loire Valley, hiked in the Alps, and saw *My Fair Lady* in London with the original cast. I got so hooked on Europe that I didn't want to go home. Casting about, I landed a job as a reporter/desk man for United Press International in Frankfurt and put in for an overseas discharge. On my last day in the Army, I needed the company clerk's signature and got in line behind a squad of new recruits. Seeing me, the clerk said, "Come up here, Bridges, and I'll give you your discharge. Then I'll take care of the rest of these guys." The recruits stared at me, bug-eyed. A man with ultimate influence! It was my proudest moment in the military.

Max Nichols inspects the troops in Würzburg. From left are Tom Daley, Klaus Lorenzen, Sgt. Wilson as Santa, Howie Bishop, Ted Wetzler, and Stew Waddell.

CHAPTER 2

Liebe zu München

Klaus Lorenzen, my Army buddy and deserter from the Hitler Youth, could never understand my love for Munich. To Klaus, whose home was Flensburg near the Danish border, the Bavarian capital was a garish stage set, with bad memories of Brown Shirts and braggadocio. There is a 1914 photo of a crowd on the Odeonsplatz celebrating the start of World War I. A wild-eyed young *fanatiker* turns out on closer inspection to be Adolf Hitler.

Klaus was no dummy. After a day or two of hurling pop-bottle gasoline bombs at American tanks in Nürnberg, he left the Hitler Jugend, hiked home to Flensburg, polished his English, became an exchange student to the United States, and enlisted in the 3rd Infantry Division as a translator, to get his citizenship. I could not explain to him the lure of Munich for a white-bread Midwesterner, whose previous idea of civic splendor had been the Johnson County, Indiana, courthouse. I'm not sure I can explain it now; all I know is that I spent the three most intense days of my life there, in the summer of 1958, walking every inch of the city (it seemed), visiting every beer hall (it seemed), and wandering for hours in the oddly named English Garden with the towers of the Frauenkirche floating in the distance like a dream.

How to explain something that was a pure explosion of the senses, a poem in gilt and stucco, a divine breath of the warm

9

South? I will be quoting Keats about "the blushful Hippocrene" if I'm not careful. Beer and bratwurst played a part, but not all that big a one. So did the relief of a three-day pass from Army discipline. But mostly I was drunk with a city whose every paving stone seemed afire for me with youth and romance. I think I had a hotel room. Perhaps I slept during the 72 hours, but if so I don't remember when.

So what did I see, do, experience in those hours?

A vignette arises. I am eating roast meat and onions on a stick outside the Augustiner Keller, in a crowd. Surely no food has ever had this sharp, all-conquering smell before. Only saffron is exotic enough to explain it, though it may be merely garlic. A little later I am sitting (in my self-consciously GI civvies) in the quietest restaurant of my life, with dim light filtering through stained glass, and ordering venison for the first time from a severely correct Herr Ober. (A lot of these memories have to do with food: its smell, savor, texture. Munich is one of the world's great cities just to eat one's way through.) When not eating or drinking, I am soaking up every building, statue, strasse, store, and vista with the avidity of someone who has only three days to live. It was something, I imagine, of what a blind man feels when the operation has succeeded, the bandages come off, and the whole wild, disorienting world of sight and color bursts in upon him. Too much, too much, and never, never enough.

To get down to earthy cases, I have tried the famed Hofbräuhaus by daylight, found it pleasant, and am now back at midnight in the Schwemme—the swim, the horse pond, the blowsy basement beer hall where busty Bavarian *mädels* carry five foaming steins in each hand. I have drunk a lot of beer. A whore is working on me at the table—a nice lady, older, a bit the worse for wear, but ready to take a lonely GI to her capacious bosom. And I am not exactly averse to the idea, despite inexperience in such matters, but why would I want to go home with her when all Munich is out there to be ravished? So I temporize and evade. A man nearby—her friend, confederate, maybe just a knowing Münchner—observes to her that I'm clearly not the kind who likes pretty girls. (I know enough German to understand all this.) How to save my macho honor, or dishonor? I apologize to her, praise her beauty, but add that "jeder Mensch ist nicht so einfach"—"Every man is not so simple." What a goof I am! I half expect her to say, in my mother's old phrase, "I'm not mad, just disgusted," but she makes a wry face and goes off to greener pastures (or ones not so green).

As if to reassert my shaky manhood, I go the next afternoon to the Marienbad public pool where the girls wear next to nothing and are falling out of that. No interest in sex from them, just in getting every possible photon of sunshine onto every centimeter of bronzed Bavarian flesh.

It's a little later still in the English Garden. I've finally slowed down enough to sit on a bench near the Chinesischen Turm, an obvious GI on holiday, and contemplate the vistas of this incomparable park. A panhandler approaches with a story of needing train fare to see his dying mother in North Germany. I listen and say, "Leider nicht, Ich habe kein Geld." Nonplussed, he tells the whole story over again, and again I say no. He draws himself up in a fury and spits at me the worst thing he can think of: "You're not an American—you're a German!"

The days, the endless afternoons, are full of summer light. In the Nürnberger Bratwurst-Glockl, with its sign showing a bell made of sausages, kitchen fires burn brightly, awakening gleams in pewter plates on the walls. At the Rathaus around the corner, the figures of the Glockenspiel come out each hour to march and play their tunes. A block away, the Karl Valentin Museum holds quirky memorabilia of the great Munich folk comic. (Sometime during the three days I have seen a film with Valentin and his delicious foil, Liesl Karlstadt.) Valentin, the story goes, was dragged offstage by the Nazis after saying, "Guess what? I saw a black Mercedes today and there wasn't an S.S. man in it!" Returning after the war and prison to a tumultuous welcome, his first words on stage were, "Guess what? There *was* an S.S. man in that Mercedes!"

I have poked my head, it seems, into half the churches of Munich; the Bridgeses are a family of church crawlers. The golden baroque sunburst above the altar of St. Johann Nepomuk still dazzles me. I have been to the zoo—Hellabrun,

11

"bright fountain"—where a woman has left her baby with me for an hour until I wonder if I've become an involuntary father. I have been past the German Museum, the Alte Pinakothek art museum, the Hofgarten. I have drunk coffee in the Café Annast on the Odeonsplatz. The Oktoberfest must wait for another visit, with Klaus this time, but I have argued with an unregenerate Nazi in the Pschorrbräu at midnight and pissed against the wall of the Maximilianeum at 2 a.m., hoping no policeman was watching.

I have also bought a little book, just published, by Wilhelm Hausenstein, titled *Liebe zu München*—"Love to Munich." The chapters are evocative: "The City and Its Panorama," "Meaning and Destiny of the City," "Of Art and Artists." Despite my limited German, I can see that these little essays are really love letters. The author's knowledge and his sensitivity to the city far exceed mine; I have adopted his title for this essay with humility and gratitude.

In the years since my three-day visit, I've returned to Munich several times, though never with the lover's first crazy passion. I spent a happy day once showing the city to a plump little New Yorker who had stopped off on her way to a kibbutz in Israel. I made an appointment long in advance with a friend to meet in the Bratwurst-Glockl at a date and time certain. I was there, he wasn't, the more loss to him.

I have worked in Munich as a reporter for an international news service, covering a horrible plane crash that also incinerated a streetcar full of Münchners. I have spent an afternoon listening to a brass quintet in an obscure suburb, and have drunk beer at dawn with farmers in the Viktualienmarkt, not an especially good idea.

I once spent most of a day going from shop to shop trying to buy an air-pressure gauge that would tell my spelunking brother how deep he was in a cave. I had to invent a vocabulary: "Tiefenmesser," depth gauge, and "Höhlewanderer," cave explorer. I may have told some startled clerks that my brother was wandering in Hell and needed to know how far down he was. But everyone listened, tried to help, walked me to the next block to point out a store that might have such a bizarre device.

I never found one, but would not have missed for the world that day in Munich among wonderful Münchners.

Eventually I took my wife and children to Munich, and I believe they loved it nearly as much as they did Venice, Paris, or London. But how to tell them what it was like to be young, with all the world before me, in the city of my dreams? Can it ever be explained, by anybody? Only years later, when I read Baron Corvo's anthem of praise and hopeless passion for Venice, did I understand what had happened to me during those three days in Munich: that my soul had been jerked clean out of my mouth and made to encompass a city, a country, a world.

And what was the city, the country, the world of Munich? Yes, it was a stage set; when I saw the repeating sandstone façades along Ludwigstrasse near the Theatinerkirche (the Theater Church!), I knew what Klaus meant. Yes, it spawned the Nazis and is next door to Dachau. It is huge and beery and vulgar. It has also been Germany's center of art, music, film, journalism, science, debate. Yeats was right about how close the places are of creation and excrement.

After a highway altercation, a Berlin truckdriver sued a Münchner for saying, "You slob, we had culture in Bavaria when you Berliners were still eating acorns in the woods." A judge threw out the case on the ground that truth was a defense. Munich was the capital of a slightly mad kingdom, and it has never forgotten. In my three days there I experienced for the first time a coherent world—what a great human city really is, a true *Weltstadt*. Munich took me in her arms, and if the embrace at times was that of a whore in the Schwemme, I knew there was pure gold in her heart.

New Year's party with Bill, Gisela Schmidtke, and an uniden-
tified reveler. Gisela's mother was an employee of our office.

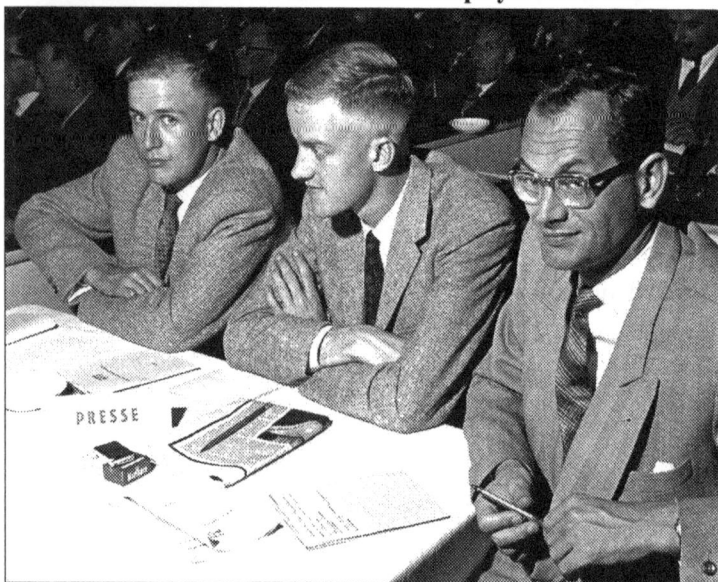

Klaus Lorenzen, Bill, and Herr Könighaus of the *Main Post* at
a Würzburg meeting of Chancellor Konrad Adenauer's party.

CHAPTER 3

WAB of UPI

It was a late summer afternoon in 1959, and I was trying out for a job with United Press International in Frankfurt, West Germany, doing rewrites from the shaky English of Stojan Bralovic, UPI's Belgrade correspondent. John Parry, the bureau manager, walked past.

"Get out to Rhine-Main Airport," he said. "Willy Brandt is coming in from the disarmament talks in Geneva. Find out what happened. Oh, and don't worry, he speaks English."

This was it. The UPI challenge. Throw the recruit into the pool with the sharks and see if he can fight his way to shore. Willy Brandt was the mayor of West Berlin and a major national figure. I grabbed a taxi to Rhine-Main, scurried through the terminal (no security then), and reached the tarmac just as Brandt and his party were descending from their plane. I walked up to him:

"Bridges from UPI. What happened in Geneva?"
"I was interviewed there. I don't know that I can add anything."
"But, but, Herr Brandt, maybe just a few words . . . ."

I was so clearly desperate, my whole future at stake, that the great man stopped and gave me some information and quotes. I wrote half a dozen paragraphs, which were never published, and got the job. That was the start of a 15-month career as what I have sometimes grandly styled "foreign correspondent." I was one, of course, but much of the work was routine drudgery, minding the American desk and grinding out copy in UPI's third-floor offices several blocks from the center of Frankfurt. For hilarious details of life in UPI, read *The Kansas City Milkman* (also titled *Dateline:Paris*) by Reynolds Packard. It will be on the fiction shelf, but it's really a documentary, particularly the part where the hero resigns by telegram: "Quitting. Pay too low. Hours too long. Life too short."

I didn't care. I *loved* working 85 hours a week with no overtime pay (actually that happened only once). The staff was a joy: John Parry, the dashing young bureau chief and sophisticate; John Callcott, Brit extraordinaire, and Karl-Heinz Mack, in charge of covering royal weddings and impersonating reporters from London tabloids, so we could horn in on their stories about vicars absconding with choirboys. Hans Shafer was our genial sports boss, who liked to talk about his days as a POW in Texas. Jerry Gilreath, also hired out of the Army, was my same-age sidekick. Don Till, a droll Englishman, ruled over photo, while the charming and beautiful Hannelore Grötsch, with other ladies, formed the pool of teletype tape punchers.

That was about it on the English-language side. We put our initials and sign-off time at the end of our stories; I was "wab," pronounced "wahb." I learned a new vocabulary: "flash," "bulletin," "sap" for "soon as possible," "sappest" for even sooner. The Associated Press, further downtown, was rumored to have dozens of reporters, but *we* were UPI—better writers, harder workers, more dedicated newshawks, each of us able to outrun, outjump, outwrite, and outfinagle any six competitors. It was an illusion that UPI management, always tight with a buck, was happy to foster.

The memories of old newsmen assume a sameness—the big stories, the scoops, the unpublishable anecdotes—and the reader will certainly not escape these here. But a news service is also a school in working quickly and accurately, writing concisely, and overcoming obstacles. Our main customers were afternoon papers in the United States, where it was seven to 10 hours earlier. Our days began slowly in the mornings, revved up in early afternoon, and sometimes (on a big story) extended far into the night. In late afternoon or early evening, we wrote an "overniter" on the day's main story. This was a wrap-up with a new intro, or "lead," for early afternoon papers in the United States. The overniter was mostly old news, but we had to make it look new. (This schedule was somewhat arbitrary. UPI liked to claim that it had, somewhere, "a deadline every minute.")

On one big story (a U.S. artillery squad had overshot in practice and killed more than 20 GIs), we had worked frantically all day, exhausting every angle as well as ourselves. At midnight there was nothing left to say, until a visiting UPI pro, Henry Keys, suggested a bit of a new slant. I wrote it with my last breath. "Great new angle," UPI London replied. "Have sent it to U.S. as new nitelead. Please produce new overniter."

We were always picturing a U.S. editor holding up our story against the AP's and deciding which to use. Management kept track of the "play" and sent us the results. Once in a while a packet of clippings arrived, with our bylined articles from the New York dailies. Fame! AP, a cooperative with member papers, had a reputation for solid competence. UPI was felt to be more colorful, and we tried to oblige with sparkling leads and snazzy writing. I wrote widely played stories about an Army colonel whose six-year-old son, dressed in full uniform with a swagger stick, followed him through the barracks on inspections, bawling out the troops. Some of them complained, and U.S. editors (former enlisted men?) ate up my "pint-sized colonel" stories. No doubt I ruined daddy's career, but he had it coming. I was an enlisted man myself.

Frankfurt was the hub of UPI operations east of Paris, with teletype or telex copy coming in from Scandinavia, Italy, Zurich, and other points. We had no direct line to Moscow, so copy on the Francis Gary Powers U-2 spy trial was dictated to Helsinki and sent down the line to us. (I was dressed down by London for being away from the desk and causing a delay in two "bulletins.") We also transmitted results from the Rome Olympics, and occasionally news of interest to Africa or South America. I had a revelation about how economics influences the news. UPI did little with the first uprisings against Portuguese rule in Africa. Henry Keys explained that we had good clients in Lisbon. If things really blew up, he said, we would cover them.

I was sent to West Berlin (this was *before* the Wall) to give Joe Fleming, the legendary Berlin bureau chief, a few days off. An eager beaver, I ran around the city, including the east sector, writing features and trying to get myself arrested by the *Volkspolizei*, who ignored me. I found the only nightclub in East Berlin. "I take my hat off to you, President Wilson," Joe said, which I took to be a line from an old song and his way of telling me I was too big for my britches, which I was. Joe suspected Wellington "Bill" Long, the excellent German manager, of sending me to Berlin to undermine him. I had no interest in that, but there *was* a huge feud going on, with Long trying to oust Fleming from the cozy niche he had occupied since postwar days. Long had a snowy mane, which people said made him look like a senator. "A *state* senator," Joe growled. Letters flew, with Joe dropping copies to top UPI executives. "Have I missed anybody?" he wrote on one. He kept his job.

In Berlin, I covered a Billy Graham Crusade that began several blocks from the East-West border, but moved for its finale to a field next to the old Reichstag, nearly on the line. Graham's publicity man had observed our fascination with the evangelist's appearance on the doorstep of godless Communism. Before the Reichstag rally, he phoned to say, "Don't miss it. We'll be even *closer* to the Iron Curtain."

I also learned in Berlin about the perfidy of business managers. UPI's cut-rate hotel, the Savoy, was filled, and I ended up at the Hilton. Dieter Schmidt, the Frankfurt money man, found out and told me to try the Savoy again. I thought of ignoring him—the Hilton had room service—but Hoosier honesty won out. "Oh, yes," the clerk at the Savoy said. "Herr Schmidt has already called and reserved your room for you."

A story of mine in October, 1960, shows how stories were handled. Under the rubric "Urgent" at 8:42 p.m. came three paragraphs headed "First nitelead Berlin" and beginning:

BERLIN, Oct. 4 (UPI) — East Berlin indicated today it considers West Germany and West Berlin two separate states whose trade is subject to Communist control.

The "indication" was in a speech by Walter Ulbricht, East Germany's leader. This was followed by an "add first nitelead" at 8:55, and third, fourth, and fifth "first niteleads" at 9:06, 9:28, and 9:56, totaling 24 short paragraphs in about an hour, which then segued back into an earlier "nitelead Berlin." The construction of the story is informative. Mayor Willy Brandt several days before had warned of possible new trade restrictions on West Berlin. Ulbricht's remarks, buried deep in a speech, seemed to suggest this also. I put the two together with a lot of background to craft a story that pointed toward a possible crisis. The "indicated" in the first paragraph was a tip-off that I was about to do a little blue-sky prognosticating.

After work, a West Berlin staffer, Felix Kittel, showed me the city's night life—a little nervously since he was married and out of the bar scene. We stopped briefly at the California Bar, which featured waitresses in garter belts, as well as cubicles at the back that probably were not used for writing letters home. Then we went on to the Resi Bar, a vast room with phones between the tables and a "water organ" that sent up jets of colored spray in time to music. Felix and I talked briefly with a couple of nice Berlin girls, and I exchanged names with one. We never met again, but somehow her name, Rita Fuhrmann, has stayed with me ever the decades.

UPI also sent me to Leipzig, in East Germany, to cover its annual trade fair. The fair was interesting, but the city was faded, depressing, and plastered with propaganda banners. A feature of the week was a Bach concert in the church where the composer had been choirmaster. We journalists noted that the musical selections seemed to balance the ideas of freedom and submission to authority, so we wrote stories about the apparent political savvy of the concert's organizers. We didn't know they were savvy, we hadn't interviewed them, it was just a bit of hype. Moreover, I was beginning to doubt some Cold War verities. At the hotel in Leipzig, I had breakfast with journalism students from the university. They were great kids—my age— and dedicated to the ideals of state journalism. "Why do you in the West slant everything?" they asked. We, slant? Just because we occasionally referred to Walter Ulbricht as "the spade-bearded dictator of East Germany"?

Other things shook my settled opinions. On the train home from Leipzig, an East German woman saw that I was from the shiny and prosperous West. "We're the bad Germans over here," she said. "We *lost* the war." In Osnabrück, doing a series on the British Army of the Rhine, I found that the Brits didn't worry as much about pleasing their neighbors as the U.S. Army had. They had taken over a soccer field, and the Germans raised a sign outside saying, "Why can't we have our field back?" Some Tommies went over with a bucket of paint and wrote, "Because we won the bloody war."

Jerry Gilreath and I teamed up for some stories, including the romantic tale of Gloria Vanderbilt's daughter, who had fallen for an American airman. Mrs. Vanderbilt, a wise mother, moved with her daughter into an apartment near Wiesbaden air base to get better acquainted with the prospective fiancée. The press descended, but Jerry—oozing southern charm—talked his way into the family circle, and we beat out everybody.

UPI, as a straight commercial operation, had to "sell the service" to stateside clients. We played host now and then to visiting publishers and on one occasion to a North Carolina trade delegation that felt being entertained should include being supplied with women. Jerry and I were asked to help, but we had enough trouble finding girls for ourselves. Norbert Sakowski of the UPI German Service sighed and took on the mission. He came in next morning fuming; one of the North Carolinians had tried to put moves on *him.*

What did it all mean? For single guys in their 20s—and they were mostly guys, with a few legendary women—it was an adrenalin rush, a chance to craft words and send them flying around the world, the matching of competitive wits. But there was also a disconnect between the "foreign correspondent" and the often lonely 24-year-old who was Bill, not "wab."

And the job could be troubling at times. I covered the court-martial of a young lieutenant who took the fall for the artillery accident. A high-ranking officer appeared as a mitigation witness, baring his soul about a similar accident that had almost blighted his own early career. We reporters, moved for once, caucused and agreed to withhold the officer's name. But one of us broke the name immediately, and I got a stern lecture

20

from UPI London not to make such agreements, even for humanitarian reasons. A tough lesson in a tough business.

There is still an organization bearing the UPI name, but it has little resemblance to the old worldwide news service. Economics, mismanagement, and a changing media world did the old company in.

A final snapshot: "UPI London to Frankfurt: Need German man-on-street reaction sappest to Russian space shot" (or plane crash or change in governments). It's midnight, there are no men on the street coherent enough to have a reaction. Hans Shafer sits and types: "Heinrich Blickendorf, Frankfurt crossing sweeper, said today that . . . ."

* * *

FRANKFURT (UPI) — It was great fun. No regrets. No new overniter.

(wab)

Hannelore Grötsch and Jerry Gilreath, of the UPI staff, at a New Year's party in Frankfurt.

21

INTERVAL: THE 'FENDERS'

One of my favorite UPI stories was about the Fenders, an alleged organization dedicated to honoring the underdogs, or "fenders," who got all the mud from "big wheels." I say alleged because it was never quite clear if the Fenders really existed outside the brain of a spokesman, who could not be identified because that would have made him a "wheel" and thus ineligible for membership. The Grand Garage of the Fenders was said to be located in a U.S. Army office in Frankfurt.

I let none of this vagueness stop me from churning out 18 inches of copy about the Fenders and saying that the organization had spread around the world among both soldiers and civilians. The Fenders reportedly even had a member in China.

The Grand Garage, I was told, presented an annual Fender-of-the-Year Award to some prominent person who had had an especially bad 12 months taking the guff for a superior. (In recent years, I imagine, Colin Powell would have been a shoo-in.)

Memberships cost $1.25, which went for letterhead stationery, for the annual award, and for pins, which had to be worn inside the lapel. Flaunting one's pin might lead to expulsion from membership, the spokesman explained. Applications could be sent to the Top Fender at a U.S. military address, although (for the usual reason) he could not be identified.

I managed to write the entire story without giving a name, until near the end when I noted that Maj. William C. Burns of Little Rock, Ark., and Capt. Theodore P. Fox of Glen Burnie, Md., had founded the Fenders "during a particularly dismal field maneuver." But no one knew where Burns and Fox were these days, the story said.

You may have noticed that I've referred only to a "spokesman" and have used masculine pronouns. That's because the Fenders barred women from membership. "Every woman is a wheel," my spokesman said.

So did I pony up my $1.25 and become a Fender? Sorry, I'm not allowed to tell you.

CHAPTER 4

Enter Elvis

All journalists have stories of the famous and powerful they have covered. Or the unique: a friend likes to tell of interviewing Eiffel Plasterer, the world's leading soap-bubble collector. I am no exception, and three celebrities from UPI days—Elvis Presley, Judy Garland, and Marlene Dietrich—come quickly to mind. (There were others on a somewhat lower level, like the Argentine economics minister, Gov. G. Mennen "Soapy" Williams of Michigan, and the top fork-lift truck operator of the U.S. 7th Army.)

Now I have to confess that I never actually interviewed Elvis, who was serving as an Army draftee in Germany and not speaking to the press. This did not, however, stop UPI from covering him. When he died in 1977, I wrote an account for the Louisville *Courier-Journal*, focusing on "the notebook"—a thick black binder in the Frankfurt UPI office that chronicled the career of draftee No. 53310761.

The notebook was our Bible, both the revealed Word and the Apocrypha. Into it went every news story sent out about Elvis, every scrap of information that could be gleaned about him, and an immeasurable residue of rumor and joyous invention.

After a while the notebook took on a life of its own, more real than the legendary private first class driving his Jeep around Friedberg Army Base a few miles away or relaxing after duty in his off-base home at Bad Nauheim.

Was it true that German girls scrawled love notes on the fence around Elvis's house? Did they arrive in early-morning squads to wash and wax the singer's BMW before he left for the day's duty at Friedberg?

The notebook said so, based on the testimony of reliable reporters. But the origin of those stories and others grew as tangled and mythic as an ancient saga. The notebook became a primary source, not only for those of us in the bureau but also for visiting magazine writers, representatives of the foreign press, and journalistic gypsies of uncertain persuasion.

One who labored for a day over the notebook, copying information for his story, discovered that some of what he was copying had been stolen from his own earlier stories.

"The longer I'm in this business," he said, "the more convinced I am that it's one big case of larceny."

Elvis gave no major interviews that I recall during his months in Germany. The closest most reporters ever came to him was a telephone chat with Col. Tom Parker, his manager.

In fact, Elvis created rather little news in Germany. He did his job, lived quietly off post with his father, grandmother, and Colonel Parker, and kept his nose clean in good-soldier fashion. The off-post ménage was strictly by the numbers; because the family members with whom he lived were "dependent" on him, his case was officially no different from that of any enlisted man living with his wife downtown "on the economy."

With no real news, reporters spent a lot of time trying to document Elvis's love life, and their titillations piled up in the notebook. A Berlin starlet occupied his attention for a while, and there was Priscilla Beaulieu, the 14-year-old daughter of an Air Force captain at Wiesbaden. The notebook reported that Elvis had showered her with expensive watches, and it may have been so. That could have been an early signal of serious affection, for, years after he left the Army, Elvis married her.

The press also kept anxious watch on reports of accidents to Elvis and on his health. When he entered a Frankfurt Army hospital with a scratchy throat, we worried right along with Colonel Parker and relaxed, sighing, when he was safely back in the barracks. Elvis's medical history went into the notebook.

24

The German press sent us scrambling for typewriters one morning with a front-page report that Elvis had appeared in a Frankfurt nightclub and performed for a mob of screaming youngsters. Barely in time, we realized what day it was—April 1. Those fun-loving Germans.

In the *Courier-Journal* files after Elvis's death, I found an Elvis story written by a *C-J* reporter on vacation in Europe in 1959. The phrases had the old ring, but the reporter was more enterprising than most. He apparently had managed to talk with Elvis and had gotten to Bad Nauheim early enough in the morning to catch a bevy of girls posed in adoring attitudes around Elvis's sports car.

They weren't washing and waxing, but surely they had been moments before. Would the notebook lie?

* * *

I did interview Judy Garland, with other reporters, when she came through Europe in 1960, performing and campaigning for John F. Kennedy. She gave a concert and met with the press; I remember that the young *New York Times* correspondent was almost too overcome to ask a question. But what I remember most is Miss Garland's nervousness in the interview, a seeming revelation of her shyness and fragile ego. That didn't keep her from singing "Over the Rainbow" as if for the very first time.

* * *

My brush with actress and singer Marlene Dietrich was more complex. She was making her first tour of Germany since leaving her homeland during the early Nazi years. She had toured the world for U.S. troops in wartime, and we didn't know how German audiences would respond to her return. (They loved her.) She was booked to sing for a military audience in Wiesbaden, and we had heard that the performance would be officers-only. I placed a call to her publicity agent, and late that night the phone in the UPI bureau rang. It was Marlene herself. I gulped and got out my question—would enlisted men be barred from her concert? There was a moment's silence, and then a growling "Hell, no! I'll sing for *everybody*," with that famous, smoky, sexy voice coming down the phone line at me like a rasp through the heart. I was nearly as overcome as the *New York Times* man by Garland.

Another reporter, Zander Hollander, and I covered the concert, which was going well until near the end when Marlene—apparently blinded by lights—fell off the stage into the orchestra pit. Before shock could give way to pandemonium, she reappeared, crawling up the steps to the stage. She got to the mike and finished the concert, but she had broken her collarbone, and that was the end of the tour. Zander and I did our news duties, then went out to a basement bar, where we found the dancers from the show giving their own impromptu and uninhibited performance. At that moment they were young, beautiful, and stars themselves. They weren't giving a thought to Dietrich.

(Zander, who was Jewish, had his own celebrity story, an odd one. He had worked in Washington and gotten to know George Lincoln Rockwell, the American Nazi leader. Rockwell seemed to like him, was even chummy, but once in a while there would be a disquieting telephone call. Rockwell phoned one day to tell him, "Zander, they are making me chairman of the Joint Chiefs of Staff, and you, my friend, are one step nearer the gas chamber.")

There is a little personal sequel to the story about Marlene Dietrich. Long afterward, in 2000, I was in a bookstore in Inverness, Scotland, and picked up a new Dietrich biography. Checking the index, I found a short report of the Wiesbaden episode, which minimized its seriousness and said Marlene had simply stumbled against some scenery while leaving the stage. Taking a slip of paper, I wrote, "No! She fell into the orchestra pit. I was there!" Then I slipped the note into the book and put the book back on the shelf, with its little anonymous bonus for the eventual buyer.

There were other interesting interviews, but the one I remember most was with the champion fork-lift truck operator. I was doing this to "sell the service"—some publisher in the

United States had promised to subscribe to UPI if we could produce a story about a hometown boy overseas. The young GI was hell-on-wheels with a fork-lift truck, but totally inarticulate. It was one of the toughest interviews I ever did.

In the Germany of 1960, despite occasional celebrity moments, being a footloose journalist was starting to pall for me. I wasn't getting to travel for pleasure, as I had hoped. Life outside work was drab, and UPI provided only occasional social interludes. The male staffers bowled at a skittles alley near the office. Frau Grötsch invited Jerry and me to a New Year's get-together. During a party at John Parry's, Don Till's wife, Isobel, sat on my lap, which would have endeared her to me even if she hadn't already been feeding me home cooking at their house in Heusenstamm.

The Frankfurt bar scene didn't appeal much. I visited "Die Sexualische Schnitte" ("The Sexual Slice"), which didn't live up to its name. I bar-hopped with a new reporter, a huge man who, with drink, became belligerently anti-German. I learned to gauge the hostility in the room and get out just before the police arrived. The woman problem continued. An exotic dancer of whom I had high hopes stood me up. Would I ever get married, have a family? Was I going about this the right way? Some of my old demons were coming back—loneliness, anxiety. I spent a lot of time eating alone in restaurants and walking around the city, feeling depressed. I talked to a chaplain at the American military hospital, who asked if I wanted to be hospitalized; when I said no, he suggested reciting the 23rd Psalm regularly. That actually helped some.

Crossing a Frankfurt street, the Zeil, one day, I decided to go home. The *Vincennes Sun-Commercial* in my hometown agreed to hire me for the same salary as UPI—$75 a week, which was fairly princely on the German economy but not much above poverty in Indiana. The UPI staff gave me a nice sendoff, and Bill Long wrote a great letter of recommendation. Henry Keys paid me a news-service compliment. "I always took you for a professional no-placer," he said. But here, for once, Henry was wrong. I needed a place, although I wasn't sure yet where it would be. On the final leg home, the bus passed through Worthington, a forlorn small town in central

Indiana. "My God, did I leave Europe for this?" I thought. Many things lay ahead, of course, and one of them—amazingly, inexplicably—was true love. But before getting to that, there is a last and personal German story to tell.

At UPI in Frankfurt: From left, reporter Dick Leonard, teletype operator Karen Fischer, and "royals" reporter Karl-Heinz Mack.

CHAPTER 5

Ruthchen

We parted more than 40 years ago, her red-bloused arm waving farewell from the apartment window at 374 Eschersheimerlandstrasse in the great city of Frankfurt am Main. She is probably dead now—I cannot think of her as old—and I find for the first time that I can write about her and about our few months together. But first a picture, ein kleines Bild, bitte.

Ruth, Ruthchen, little Ruth, who was anything but little, being a stocky and strapping woman, in her early 30s to my 24, an older woman. My landlady, at the top of the second flight of stairs in a vast cinderblock apartment building. Ruth, with an open, round face and a voice full of broad mirth that could turn in a moment to exquisite sarcasm. A survivor of the war, mother of a mulatto 10-year-old, Ollie, fathered on her by Oliver, Sr., of the occupying U.S. Army, a child with few prospects in a country not friendly to the by-blows of American GIs, and certainly not to those of color.

There is a snapshot, probably taken by Ruth, of Ollie and me posing outside our apartment building. There are no photos of Ruth and me, and I tore up, on the boat home, the portrait she gave me of herself. Tore it up out of love and hopelessness, knowing we would never see each other again, and that I had to leave her entirely, even in memory. Or so I thought then, with the foolishness and self-pity of youth.

There should also be a description of me, and let it be a true and uncompromising one. An ex-GI discharged in Germany and working as a reporter and desk man for United Press International on Kurt-Schumacherstrasse in Frankfurt. Self-centered, ambitious, vain of my writing, repressed but wild for women. Carrying a mild load of loneliness and depression much of the time. Skinny with broken teeth. A generally unattractive case, except to an Irish Catholic teacher at the American school, whom I would have gone to bed with had not her faith, and her own standards, required my becoming a husband first. When it became clear I was a candidate, I ran like a rabbit, back to Ruth and Ollie and our four-room-and-bath menage à trois.

Let there be a picture also of the apartment. An outside door opening into a small and dingy hall, with a narrow kitchen and a bath branching from the left, Ruth and Ollie's rumpled bedroom at the end, a dusky parlor next to it. Then back down the other side of the hall to my room, just inside the front door, with windows opening on the street. Old battered furniture throughout, everything a bit dusty, Ruth being no housekeeper. Ruth being . . . . what? Of fixed abode, but uncertain provision. I was the latest in a series of roomers, following a man described vaguely as involved with airlines. The room was rented illegally, since Ruth paid no tax on it. A nondescript boyfriend appeared from time to time—Eric, pronounced "Erichhh," the name given a rich roll of the tongue by Ruth. He may have paid some of the expenses, and Ollie's father in America may have paid others. There may also have been a bit of something else; Ruthchen had a sugar daddy somewhere and disappeared now and then for several days, leaving Ollie with a friend.

It was, one may imagine, not quite the place my midwestern parents, broad-minded for the 1950s, would have chosen for their eldest son. Scratching out letters in my room, I edited my life, referring occasionally to my "landlady," the term implying an aged and safe frowsiness.

And yet, and yet . . . . . how little scandalous there would have been to tell. I may have lusted after my Irish schoolteacher or Margaretta DeLour, who danced *au naturel* in a

downtown bar to "The Spanish Washerwoman." But Ruth was
. . . . home. Even her occasional appearances in bra and panties
were domestic and curiously sexless events. Eric and the sugar
daddy took up her energies, not the pale lodger in the front
room. Instead of going to bed, we went to the movies, or saw
the Balkan dancers, or took Ollie to a Russian circus. We met
in the kitchen over supper, exchanged the day's news, washed
the dishes. At Easter I hid candy eggs for Ollie in the parlor,
concealing a couple of them in my ears, to his delight.

Without our noticing it, friendship came. And with it
heartache. One night in the kitchen, Ruth confessed that she
was pregnant by Eric, a diagnosis confirmed by a furtive doctor
who borrowed my bedside lamp for his examination. No doubt
he was also the abortionist who landed Ruth in a hospital, in
danger of death or criminal prosecution. She escaped both, but
it took money, some of it mine slipped into Eric's damp hand,
to pull her through. Let pro-lifers and pro-choicers debate. I
would have said I hated the idea of abortion . . . but this was
Ruth, and so I faced for the first time the contest between a
principle and a human being for whom I cared, and made a
choice.

She was merry again soon, sarcastic and teasing. Having
found me a soft touch, she and Eric might have taken advan-
tage, but no such thing happened. I realize now that Ruth was
an intensely, if spasmodically, moral person. We were friends,
we lived together, I was off limits. She never asked me for anything, even indirectly.

Using my mother's Christmas money from home, I bought
her a winter coat, to replace her old shabby one. And without
our noticing, something very like love slipped in. We com-
forted each other, stood by each other, made a home together in
the storm rack of our lives.

In a few months it ended, in the way of such stories. One
day I decided, between one side of a street and the other, to go
home. Ruth and I kissed goodbye, and she waved from the
window as I boarded the streetcar, her red blouse a vivid flag
against the cinderblocks. In a garden in Amsterdam, waiting for
the boat, I began to weep and couldn't stop. But I got on the

31

boat, and in misery and longing tore up the photo she had given me.

This is not quite the end of the story, and the ending is painful to tell, because it does not reflect well on the teller. There were one or two letters, and finally one from Ruth that was an unmistakable love letter. And I answered with my own letter, but in a foolish and unfeeling way that I now know was unforgiveable, because I was not going back, because I had not told her I loved her when it would have counted, because my cold sense of self-preservation kept me from it. She never wrote again.

"But that was in another country . . . ." Regret is a futile emotion, and the story is an old one; we would have been a disaster as anything more than what we were. I tore up your photo, Ruth, but you have stayed in my heart these 40 years, unforgettable. I write this now, belatedly, at the other end of life, out of gratefulness for your spirit, your sharp tongue, your honor . . . . and your love.

Bill and Ollie

CHAPTER 6

The Love and Marriage Part

Gather around me, children, and I will tell you how your mother and I met, fell in love, married, and produced your astonishing selves. Everyone comfy? Then let's begin. When I met Karen, your mother-to-be, she was beautiful, vibrant, smart, funny, and incredibly sexy. Wow! Let me tell you . . . .

Karen: Now wait just one little minute here . . . .

Me: Hey, that's how I remember it. Write your own memoirs.

* * *

Okay, so this approach isn't working. Let's try the rigidly factual one.

SCENE ONE

I met Karen Ann Petersen, age 19, about 1 p.m. on Aug. 21, 1961, in the office of Maxine Batman, head of the Vincennes, Indiana, Public Library. I was a much-traveled and world-weary 26. Miss Petersen had just been hired as a junior librarian, and I, reporter that I was for the *Vincennes Sun-Commercial*, had been assigned to interview her. It was a slow news day.

Karen: Watch it, Buster.

Me: Okay. But I did make a good impression, didn't I, because I spelled Petersen with the correct Danish "e," not "o" like those other Scandihoovians?

Karen: It was a point in your favor.

Me: And then, moving with blinding speed, on May 25 of the following year, I asked you for a date.

Karen: Yes, it was my father's birthday, and we had cake with my folks and then went go-karting in Westport, across the Wabash in Illinois.

Me: I carried you across the state line?

Karen: Yes, but for depressingly moral purposes.

Me: And you kept running your go-kart into the protective hay bales. Clearly you needed someone to take care of you.

Karen: You may believe that if you wish.

Me: And then we went to Wally's root-beer stand across the highway and talked.

Karen: And talked and talked.

Me: Had we had any substantive contacts between the dates of Aug. 21, 1961, and May 25, 1962? I lived across the street from the library, after all, in a house painted with giant hex symbols by the mad inventor Leonard Crowe.

Karen: You did come in a lot. And you used to call the reference desk and ask me to look up all those dumb things that nobody else in the world would care about. Why *did* you want to know if Black Beauty was a boy or girl horse?

THE LOVE AND MARRIAGE PART

Me: I forget. But it was a portent of things to come?

Karen: Yes.

Me: And how did we spend the summer of 1962?

Karen: If you don't remember, I'm not going to tell you.

Me: I do remember some things now. Like the night we were sitting in your kitchen, and you and your mom suddenly jumped up, grabbed a flashlight and gun, and ran out of the house firing.

Karen: I still can't believe you didn't hear that possum in the chicken house. City boys!

Me: Well, I had never dated anybody from the country whose parents had run a mom-and-pop truck stop and who had been raised by car-transport drivers. It was a multicultural experience. And I loved your parents. Mary was so great to me. And Fritz took me around to all his favorite drinking places in town. I can still taste those schooners at the Imperial.

Karen: The hog hearts lowered you in my mother's estimation, though.

Bill: Oh, yeah. I mentioned how good they were when my dad cut them in pieces, floured, and fried them. And she burst out, "Hog hearts? We used to feed those to the dogs!"

Karen: We announced our engagement on my 21st birthday, Sept. 16, 1962, which is also Mexican Independence Day, if you'd like a little reference-desk factoid to go with this.

Me: And I sneaked your engagement photo into the *Sun-Commercial*, giving the printers a phony name on the page dummy, a name now known (since all the printers are dead) only to us. A name that we will use only if a crazed killer is forcing one of us to make a phone call, or we are trying to communicate from beyond the grave.

Karen: Uh, what was the name again?

Me: Whatever. So we were married on Dec. 30, 1962, in the First Baptist Church of Vincennes, with the Rev. Jack Davis officiating. My Army buddy, Max Nichols, was best man, and my sister Ann was your maid-of-honor. With Max's help, we pretended to leave town, but actually spent the wedding night in our upstairs apartment at 513 Church St., before leaving next day for a wild honeymoon in Louisville and Bardstown, Ky.

Karen: Ah, you still remember those nights of passion.

Me: I remember you ate a lot.

[Sounds of slaps, screams]

Karen: I also remember that our mothers made my wedding dress (it cost about $35). Your mother did the front because she didn't do zippers, and my mother the back because she didn't do darts. I came home from Indiana University at Bloomington, tried it on, and it fit.

Me: And we lived happily ever after.

Karen: So far. But it's only been 42 years, so don't get over-confident.

Me: By the way, I've been wondering about something for 42 years. Did I ever actually *propose*? I don't seem to remember the going-down-on-one-knee part. Did I ever actually *say,* "Will-you-Karen-Ann-Petersen-marry-me-William-Arthur-Bridges?"

Karen: No, silly. We just kept talking, and pretty soon we were talking about what the wedding would be like.

Me: And you were beautiful, vibrant, smart, funny, and incredibly sexy.

* * *

SCENE TWO

[Later]

The Children: Tell us more, Daddy.

Me: Okay. Karen, have you ever, at any time, had second thoughts about the wisdom of our embarking together upon the sea of matrimony—any fears that we might have been embarking up the wrong sea?

Karen: No oftener than once a week. And there were some really nice moments, like coming out of Dr. Fred's and handing you his note with "Suspect twins." And the look on your face.

Me: Karl and David. And we went around for the 10 days until delivery holding up two fingers and grinning.

Karen: But there was also the year with two babies at the University of Missouri, when you were finishing your master's degree, and we lived in a trailer out the Mexico Gravel Road, and the big event of my week was going to Gerbe's Supermarket to buy out the baby-food section. And then there was the spouse abuse.

Me: Okay, okay—so you were storming out of the trailer because you had terminal cabin fever, just as I was coming in with flowers, and I got mad and said, "Go! And take these with you!" and threw the flowers at your back. But I did take them out of the vase first.

Karen: Yes, that was kind of sweet. But there was still "The Newspaper." I have a chapter in *my* memoirs (unwritten) that is called "How I Made My Peace With The Newspaper." It was in Hornell, N.Y., remember? You were managing editor of the *Tribune*, and I was at home with the twins and Michael on the way, and it was clear that I was playing second fiddle to the newspaper, and that the boys were barely in the orchestra. There wasn't anything I could do. I couldn't even go home to Mommy, because she had already said that if we ever split up she was taking you. So I finally decided that I loved you, and that if I had to share you with the newspaper, then so be it.

Me: But didn't we talk about it? Didn't I promise to do better?

Karen: Oh, sure. And then as soon as there was a City Council meeting, you'd be gone again. If it had been another woman, I would have known what to do. But I didn't know how to fight City Hall.

Me: But you hung in, you didn't give up, you gallant girl.

Karen: Well, I *thought* you were a smart person and might eventually figure it out.

Me: And over the ensuing 40 years have I figured it out, improved, become a more sensitive guy?

Karen: [Long pause] Yes.

* * *

SCENE THREE

[Still later]

Me: Shall we bring this to a close? The children are nodding. I'm still worrying about that long pause above.

Karen: Good, you were meant to. But you really did improve. I think it was getting involved in Cub Scouts. That was a turning point.

THE LOVE AND MARRIAGE PART

Me: And then Colin was born, and I decided to leave newspapers—it was the Louisville *Courier-Journal* by then—and become a college professor. And you got a job as a newspaper reporter, based on your previous experience covering a horse show, a fleabag circus, and a tornado—and then it was you saying, "I won't be home until midnight, dear, I have an election."

Karen: Revenge was sweet.

Me: And we traveled around the world and saw exotic places like Taipei and Japan and Scotland and Australia and the Sod House Museum in Colby, Kansas . . . .

Karen: Wait, wait—remember we also traveled when the kids were little—to Venice, Germany, Denmark, Yugoslavia—because we wanted them to see the world, too, and it was dumb to wait until we were old and creaky.

Me: "Now that we're old, and ready to go / We get to thinkin' what happened a long time ago. / We had a lot of kids, trouble, and pain / But, oh lord, we'd do it again." [CHORUS] "She had kisses sweeter than wine. / She had (oh, oh) kisses sweeter than wine."

Karen: How do you remember that stuff? But, yes.

Me: Oh, look, the boys are all asleep. Aren't they sweet?

Karen: There is nothing more beautiful than a sleeping child—unless it's four of them.

Me: Umm, I dunno. Have I mentioned lately that you're beautiful, vibrant, smart, funny, and incredibly sexy?

[Curtain closes.]

Smith Studio, Columbia

Above, Karen and Bill with David and Karl, Columbia, Mo., 1965. At left: Bill with publisher Louis Buisch at Hornell, N.Y., *Evening Tribune.*

Photo by Brad Bliss

CHAPTER 7

'It Rhymes With You and Me'

I became a newspaperman, probably, one lovely April day in 1953 when I picked my way over a field of stubble on the old Ivory Drybread farm west of Franklin, and asked a farmer to tell me how his spring plowing was coming along. The farmer stopped his tractor, got down, lit a cigarette, and told me about tilling the earth.

Things have to be just right, he said, with the frost well out of the ground and the soil ready to crumble. He picked up a clod and crumbled it—like that, he said. After 10 minutes or so, he got back on his tractor and drove off, a happy man doing what he knew and loved. I went back to the *Evening Star* and wrote about him, doing what I loved and was beginning to know just a little about.

William Carlos Williams once saw a girl crossing a street and said long afterward that all his poetry had been for her. I could say that all my work for 50 years has been for that old farmer, turning his rich furrow of earth across Ivory Drybread's acres. For him, and for all those who want to know about him and the world he and they inhabit together. A journalism student once wrote, "I want to find out things and tell people about them." I can say it no better than that.

The bare facts of a working life for most of us are so quick to tell that it hardly seems we were here. I'll get the newspaper job resumé over with in a few lines. Cub reporter, Franklin *Evening Star* and Vincennes *Sun-Commercial*, 1953-56; Army editor, 1957-9; UPI foreign correspondent, 1959-61; back to

41

reporter on the *Sun-Commercial*, 1961-64. Then there were a couple of more substantial jobs: managing editor, the Hornell (N.Y.) *Evening Tribune*, 1965-68; subeditor, Louisville *Courier-Journal*, 1968-79. Coda: a summer with Scripps Howard in Washington, 1993; senior copy editor, *Free China Journal*, Taiwan, 1993-4. Bang, I'm done.

But not quite. If there were space, I'd tell you about interviewing Mrs. John F. Kennedy—no, not *that* one, but a woman, fat and shapeless as a feed sack, who sat on a broken bench and told me how she and her family fished the Wabash River for mussels. "Pearl City," their little scatter of hovels was called, on the riverbank behind the George Rogers Clark Memorial in Vincennes. I would tell you about Daryl Baldwin, an eighth-generation descendant of the Miami chieftain Little Turtle, who has a Ph.D and is resurrecting the Miami language. I would tell you about Snoopy, the bald duck. And a little later I *will* tell you about Lorene Onstott and her cats, one of my favorite interviews.

But first let me expand on the resumé just a little. As I was finishing my master's at the University of Missouri in 1965, I placed a job ad in a trade publication. A man named Louis G. Buisch flew to Missouri and took Karen and me to dinner. He was publisher of the Hornell (N.Y.) *Evening Tribune,* a 14,000-circulation afternoon daily southwest of the Finger Lakes. He needed a managing editor, and I would do. "You'll go on to bigger things," he said, "but we'll get all we can out of you and brag about you when you're famous." Karen and I packed a U-Haul, the twins, and headed to New York.

At the end of *Tender Is the Night*, F. Scott Fitzgerald writes that Dick Diver's last post card was mailed from Hornell, N.Y., "a very small town." Hornellians still smart a little about their literary fame, and indeed they deserve better. Hornell is an old Erie railroad town, with so many nationalities that we once ran ethnic recipes for several months without repeating a country. Pie a la mode began there when a cook in the Erie depot café substituted ice cream for the usual thick dairy cream that had been lapped up by the depot cat. The delicacy worked its way down the Erie to the bon ton in New York City.

Louie Buisch was an excellent, hands-off boss, who taught me a valuable lesson. I had written a blistering memo to a habitually tardy reporter. Lou looked at it, folded it up, and said, "He's right out there in the newsroom. Why don't you go talk to him." Thanks to Lou, I have torn up a lot of memos without sending them.

I nearly worked myself and my marriage to death in Hornell. Finally, to break out of that rut and for other reasons, I quit and applied to a big-city daily, the *Courier-Journal* in Louisville, Ky. Pre-employment tests and lunch seemed to go well, and I was taken to see George Gill, the managing editor, who looked at me coldly. "You have a lot of good credentials, but I don't think we can hire you," he said. Why not, I asked. "Because," Gill said, "I'm not sure I want to hire someone who got a better score on the spelling test than I did." Then he grinned. I was in, but for a copyeditor's job rather than a reporter's, as I had expected.

It turned out that copyediting suited me even better than reporting. People who are basically shy can be fine reporters if they "want to find out things" badly enough. But in Louisville, I discovered that what I really loved was working with fine reporters to make their stories just a little better. I had learned in Hornell not to impose my own style on other writers; a copyeditor is good when a reporter knows his story has improved, but can't quite tell what the editor did. Copyeditors are anonymous and get their reward in the success of others. Or occasionally from writing a headline. Queen Elizabeth was pictured one day with one of the royal pooches, and I wrote, "Corgi and Bess." Oh, joy! Oh, rapture! Who needs a byline?

Down the street from the newspaper was Teek's World-Famous New York Bar & Grill (world-famous because a former patron had once sent Teek a post card from Europe). Over a beer, or several, city editor Chris Waddle (pronounced Wah-DELL) decided we should win a Pulitzer Prize and wrote the topic on a napkin: tobacco. It was a gutsy choice in a state where tobacco was a big crop. Chris assembled a team of the paper's best writers and assigned me as project editor, to harness egos, keep everyone pulling together, and make all the pieces fit. It was the most fascinating and demanding job of editing I'd ever had. It took months and resulted in a 20-part series that didn't win a Pulitzer but did collect other prizes. This was in the 1970s, and in a pile of research material we found the name of an obscure scientist who had found a smoking gun, so to speak, about the deadliness of tobacco.

The *C-J's* reporters, with rare exceptions, were an editor's dream. Barry Bingham had not yet sold the paper to the Gannett chain; he cherished the *C-J* and plowed money back into it. When the paper looked into buying new presses, the banks said a 2 percent profit margin wasn't enough for such a large loan. We labored to get it up to 12 percent, but there were too many good stories to be covered, and this cost money. Today, newspaper profits of 35 percent are not unusual, and publishers wring their hands over why readership is declining.

Many fine reporters passed through the *Courier-Journal* and went on to bigger things, among them Howard Fineman at *Newsweek,* Joel Brinkley at the *New York Times,* and Charles Babcock at the *Washington Post.* Also some who were never heard of again, like the one who began a story: "Joe Typical (not his real name)."

If war is diplomacy by other means, editors can be said to pursue reporting by a different path. Part of my joy in editing was helping reporters conceptualize stories and then explore the possibilities. If the story was about Ruritan clubs (Kiwanis for farmers), what really went on there? Did the members sing "Old McDonald" as their club song? (No.) Did they arrive at meetings in bib overalls with mud on their boots? (Sometimes.)

Once in a while editors even became reporters. When tornados swept through central Kentucky in 1974, Karen helped track them from home with her ham radio rig. Then she called me on the city desk, and I telephoned numbers just ahead of or behind the storm. One call was answered by a couple whose roof had been blown away as guests were arriving for a dinner party. The dining room was untouched; they ate by candlelight under the stars.

Eli Brecher, a reporter whose parents had owned the Apollo Theater in Harlem, was sent to cover some rural flooding and reported that "hoglets" were wallowing in pools left by the receding water. Hoglets? "Well, what are they?" Eli fumed.

"Swinelets? Porklets? How do you expect a good Jewish girl from New York to know things like this?"

George Gill encouraged creativity, although often with the admonition, "Good idea, but don't do it every day." One Saturday night I realized that all the stories on our secondary front page for Sunday had religion angles. So I changed the title of the "corrections" box from "Beg Your Pardon" to "Forgive Us Our Trespasses." A memo from the publisher inquired, "Have we changed our style on the corrections box?" The message to me was not "don't do it every day," but "don't do it again, ever."

The *Courier-Journal* of that era did a lot of serious and distinguished reporting, but it also allowed scope for imagination and occasional lunacy. We published an annual Kentucky Derby edition with news of race-track fashions, celebrities, and even horses, photographed from a helicopter as they sped around the track at Churchill Downs. It was "the Run for the Roses."

One year we discovered that students at a Catholic school, Spalding College, were planning a "Run for the Rodents," with mice circling a miniature track. An editor, Jerry Ryan, swindled a page of space, and the newsroom's best minds went to work on stories and photos mimicking Derby coverage. Photographer Frank Kimmell, heading for the Spalding roof, was stopped by a suspicious nun. "It's all right, Sister," he said. "I'm shooting the aerials of the race." Amazingly, the paper printed all of this.

Having mentioned inspired lunacy, I think it's time to call on Lorene Onstott. I was alone in the newsroom on the May morning after Seattle Slew won the 1977 Kentucky Derby. Then the phone rang. Here's the story that appeared next day:

A WHOLE SLEW OF KITTENS

Some people think there isn't enough good news in the paper, and Lorene Onstott and I are going to do something about it.

Nobody is going to stop us, because nobody else is up at this hour on Sunday morning after the Kentucky Derby.

Mrs. Onstott, who says she lives "in a big old Victorian house" at 4011 Southern Parkway, called the *Courier-Journal* city desk a few minutes ago to report she had stayed home from the Derby Saturday because the stray cat that had adopted her during January's blizzard was about to have kittens. Mrs. Onstott sensed motherhood approaching on Derby Eve, but went on to bed.

"I don't stay awake for kittens," she said.

Still, when mama cat was missing Saturday, Mrs. Onstott knew what had to be done. She scratched her Derby trip.

"I thought, 'I cannot go. I cannot leave her.' I crawled everywhere. Scratched my leg. It was bleeding. I finally found her in the hedge."

The kittens began arriving about Derby time, and Mrs. Onstott christened the first one after the winner, even though the kitten is yellow, and that other Seattle Slew is a glossy black.

"In my heart I knew it's Seattle Slew," she said.

Place, show, and fourth were two white kittens and a gray. A whole slew of kittens. Mrs. Onstott never intended to provide a home for even one.

"I'm a horse person, not a kitten person," she said.

When mama showed up in January, Mrs. Onstott didn't give her a name and fed her outside. But, as she said yesterday, "We don't really own them. They own us."

So now a nursery has been set up in the garage for the new mother and her family.

"She's all primped up out there with little maternity-room sheets," Mrs. Onstott said. "And Seattle Slew is sitting up there, acting like he's the prince of everything."

Is Slew a tom or a tabby?

"My golly, how would I know?" said Mrs. Onstott. Just put it in the paper. On Page 1.

"This cat deserves it, and so do I. And anyway, it's Mother's Day."

* * *

After several years as a faceless "rim rat" (on the outer edge of a horseshoe copydesk), I moved to the city desk and eventually became "day city editor," a title I liked because, with a bit of Gary, Indiana, accent, I could make it come out as, "Yes, I'm duh city editor of the *Courier-Journal.*" But when I applied for the actual city editorship, the job went to someone else. I had been on the paper 11 years, and my thoughts were turning elsewhere, including to creative writing. Could I segue to a job as an English teacher? Probably not, since I didn't know what a predicate nominative was.

But one day a call came from Harvey Jacobs, my old professor at Franklin College and now a college trustee and editor of the *Indianapolis News.* It was time to come home, he said; the college was desperate for a journalism teacher.

I applied, got the job, and gave my notice to the *C-J,* half a year before the fall term. This was a mistake. After a month or two, colleagues were asking, "Are you still here?" or "I guess the thing at Franklin didn't work out, huh?"

But when the day came, they gave me a party, a $100 gift certificate for books, and a *C-J* "front page" with stories by some of the best journalists it has been my pleasure to know. "Franklin College will close by December," read the banner headline. "Journalism first to go in cutback of 'frills.' Lack of qualified faculty cited."

* * *

In her comic novel *Cold Comfort Farm*, Stella Gibbons paraphrases Thomas Hobbes: "The life of a journalist is poor, nasty, brutish and short. So is his style." But the best journalists somehow transcend this to tell us something about ourselves and those with whom we share our astonishing blue planet.

Jay Lawrence, a talented *C-J* reporter, once wrote a moving account of a pauper burial. The dead man had lived for years in a cheap nursing home, with no money, no friends, no relatives, never a letter—as near a cipher as anyone could be. Jay told his story in words that for a brief moment made him immortal. The story was written so well that few readers noticed Jay hadn't named him. Then he did so in the last line, simply and unforgettably: "His name was Eugene Lee. It rhymes with you and me."

INTERVAL: AN EXPERT

On a fall day in 1969, Alan B. Cole sat on his cot in a run-down rooming house in Hornell, N.Y., and talked about Boston rockers. He seemed desperately poor and sick, but he knew a vast amount about chair making.

He told me he had begun learning the furniture-finishing trade in 1906 and had risen to be a finish inspector at the world's largest piano factory. Then for 35 years he restored and refinished antiques. He had written a little manuscript about Boston rockers, which he wanted me to get published—he may have hoped to make a little money from it. I took the MS, but time passed, I moved on, Cole died.

He was an artist, who also wrote well. All the various woods used in rockers "came from the nearest farmer's wood-lot, all cut into cordwood lengths," he wrote in his *parvum opus*. "The plank for seats and other needs was sawmill stock, all air-cured (dried). No chair maker would put his reputation 'on the line' by using green woods."

Cole explained that hardwoods were always doweled into soft, not the other way around. Pine was never used, because of its high pitch content and tendency to split. After some careful description of chair measurements, Cole got to the back posts which "were made of elm and were over twice as large around as the spindles. Elm was used because its long stringy texture resists breaking across the grain. It bends easily and can be bored through and still be reliable."

"The top ends of the posts were cut back three to four inches and halfway through. The other half lapped onto the headboard, glued and fastened with two deeply countersunk flathead screws. The screwheads and countersink were plugged with coach finisher's thick, non-shrinking 'rough stuff' to secure against easy loosening. There is no other name for 'rough stuff' and its composition is no secret." (But another expert I asked recently had no idea what "rough stuff" was.)

Cole also told me that the way to assure high-quality French polish for piano finishing is to strain the liquid though an old felt hat. I hope to use this information someday.

48

CHAPTER 8

In the Strength of Our Days

Unpack the preceding chapter, reader. Try to unpack 25 years of your own life. The obituary notice will be short and (I hope) sweet, but what really happened in those days when your powers were at their height and you could have done anything—all of which did not get into the resumé or the carefully crafted letter of application?

Vietnam came and went in those years. So did six presidents, one of them assassinated. Karen and I entertained Gene McCarthy's anti-war troops in our upstate New York home—in front of our TV their faces fell as Lyndon Johnson withdrew, leaving them with no enemy to fight. From that war, I learned never again to trust a political leader; I might follow one, but it would be with eyes wide open and much skepticism.

We worked, we had kids, we bought houses. I quit jobs before finding new ones—my writing and editing pencil would always assure me of something, I thought. People came for dinner, and we went with them to watch our kids play T-ball, or gathered at backyard picnics where lighted balloons were launched into the summer evening. We traveled and camped, made yards and gardens. One spring our house sprouted with hundreds of peat pots, each with its hopeful seedling. Epiphanies happened. I saw the faces of my wife and children through the rain-smeared window of an arriving train. On a day of sun and high clouds over our garden, pure peace descended for an hour, an amazing gift.

At work, I relearned editing with some of the ferocity I had once given to Latin. This was the Big Time—a major daily newspaper, coasting a little now but rated not long since among the nation's 10 best. Karen and I went out with another editing couple—we liked them, but the man criticized and schemed so incessantly that the staff rebelled and drove him out. "You have a high tolerance for shitheads," someone told me.

I wrote some tough memos myself. One of them caught the eye of a new editor, who grilled me about just how ruthless I was prepared to be. Not enough for him, it seemed, and long afterward he came to serious grief. Another editor arrived, who was imaginative, bulky, and tough on reporters. I became his right-hand man and buffer with the staff, which called him "the Tuna." My own nickname, I discovered, was "Tuna Helper," but it seemed to be a fairly friendly one. George Buchanan, our newsroom clerk, kept the workday links up between Karen and me. In an emergency, he could always be counted on to know where I was.

Sometimes parallel lives seemed to be going on—one of domesticity and married love, the other on an edge of ambition and danger. One Christmas Eve, I edited stories about Apollo circling the moon, then was held up and robbed in the parking lot outside. A few months later, it happened again, more frighteningly. My assailant, hand suspiciously in pocket, said, "Let's find your car and take a little ride." But my car had been towed; I put on an act, ranting and cursing the police, then pushed by him and walked away, half-expecting a bullet in the back.

With Jim Adams, a reporter assigned to the "night life" beat, I toured strip bars and met his up-all-night sources. He also took me to a suburban parking lot where foes of busing for desegregation were gathering with baseball bats. "We know you tell it like it is, Jim," one of them told him. "It's them damn editors downtown who twist everything." (I tried not to look like a damn editor.) Another reporter, Merv Aubespin, took me into black Louisville, whose churches and business districts were like a foreign city, mirroring the one I knew.

I became the editor for a reporter investigating the city's prostitution. For days and at all hours, he met women in their rooms, paying their fees while he interviewed them. He talked with vice squad members and found his way to suburban housewives making extra money while their husbands worked. We met for lunch at downtown cafés and he unloaded the stories on me. When they were done, the galley proofs hung on the editor's wall for weeks, but the stories never ran. They were too racy for our family newspaper.

I wrapped up my part of the paper at midnight, then went drinking in pressmen's bars with reporters, editors, and photographers. At 2 a.m. I steered my way home carefully over the Ohio River. But once it was 5 a.m., from a party at someone's house; there was a major "domestic," in whispers so as not to wake the children, and I promised to call the next time. "I had visions of you dead in an alley," Karen said later. "And if you weren't, you were going to be."

I was innocent as the snow, but at the party I had watched astonished as a friend sexually bullied a young and vulnerable copyeditor. What people did to each other! But was I immune? At a conference, I talked with an especially kind and thoughtful woman, and later on sent her a casual note, to deepen the acquaintance. She answered just as casually. Why was I risking— even for a moment, even in my mind—real happiness for a chimera? At the end of Sean O'Faolain's short story "A Sweet Colleen," a friend surveys the naïve protagonist's tangled love life and exclaims, "Men!" And in the next breath, "Women!"

The great blizzard of 1977-78 fell on us. All traffic was suspended, but nothing could keep me from work. I started trudging over the Ohio River bridge, and luckily was picked up before I froze by a doctor with a four-wheel-drive Jeep. From work, I telephoned Karen. The paper's pilot-photographer was snowbound—she was to take our camera and walk to a parking lot near home, where a helicopter with its door removed would pick her up to shoot aerials over the paralyzed city. Although acrophobic at the time, she was bundled, padded, and ready to go ("I looked like the Michelin Man") when the regular photographer showed up. She is the heroine of my life, often a tower of strength but this time Fay Wray in the clutches of the newspaper gorilla.

Oh, reader, what forces drive us in the strength of our days, and what energies! What prodigies we perform, and what stupidities, hardly to be recollected later in tranquillity.

I was still growing up (as you may have noticed) at 40. Some shell was breaking. Its nature was unknown to me, but it seemed to have something to do with the people around me and what obligations I might have to them as fellow human beings. For a while, I threw myself into good works, serving on a church board, leading a Cub Scout pack, walking for charity. Late one night, I stopped to help strangers with a broken-down car. They were a rough lot and looked ready to take my own car, but didn't. Around me, others were settling into lifetime careers, whatever mid-life crises they might be concealing. (Well, not quite all; when I next met one of them, he was running an ocean-fish business on the East Coast!)

I had begun to suspect that some sort of clock was running. With every job had come a point of restlessness, a need to move on, though there was always some other excuse. Each time something had rescued me from the finality of comfortable success—this time, although it would take a while, the rescuer would turn out to be poetry.

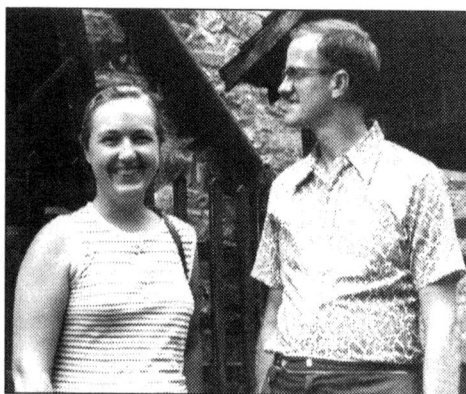

CHAPTER 9

And Now, Poetry

I published my first poem at age 11, under a pseudonym, in the "Hoosier Homespun" column of the *Indianapolis News.* It was short, and I remembered it as not too bad—kids are sometimes good natural poets. A 30-year writer's block followed, broken only by occasional valentine verses to my wife. I was a journalist, a writer of prose. It wasn't that I didn't like poetry—I had memorized lots of florid verse in school—but other people wrote that, people with poetic imaginations.

Venice shocked me out of that idea. My family and I went there in 1974, as a sort of celebration of Karen's long-delayed college graduation. We fell in love with the city, even though it was cold and rainy and I had told everybody to leave their raincoat liners at home. They've never let me forget it. "We still remember freezing our butts off in the piazza outside St. Mark's," Karen says. I had read extensively before going and had drawn a map of the city in chalk on our kitchen wall. My Uncle Stephen, an artist and Venetophile, had pumped us full of what to do and see and had recommended his own hotel, Paganelli's, on the Riva degli Schiavoni just down from the Royal Danieli. So we had a great time, and David even found a Venetian angler who loaned him a pole to fish in the Grand Canal.

A few weeks after returning, I realized that Venice had gotten to me. I had to write something, and prose was inadequate. I found myself writing a little four-stanza poem that began:

> *Bright city in the sea, the night*
> *brings messengers who softly go*
> *up liquid latticeways of light*
> *by silent sandolo.*

Not so great, all that sibilance and liquefaction. But I had written a poem! So I wrote a few more, all of them about Venice, each getting progressively worse. But it didn't matter; poetry had gotten me by the throat, and suddenly nothing else seemed half as worth doing. (That discovery coincided, as I've mentioned, with the desire to leave the news business and do something more creative.) I did have the good sense to realize that I needed help, and began seriously reading and thinking about what good poets did. I read John Ciardi's book *How Does a Poem Mean?* which was a great help. I began keeping a notebook, which at first was mainly a place to copy down poems I liked. The first was Louise Bogan's "A Tale," which begins:

> *This youth too long has heard the break*
> *Of waters in a land of change.*
> *He goes to see what suns can make*
> *From soil more indurate and strange.*

Mysterious, spare, and beautiful language. Bogan still dazzles me. Several of her lyrics are among the best in English, in my opinion. Bogan was also a help in moments of frustration. She had written to Ted Roethke: "They [the leaves] fell and fell and a brook murmured, and I sat on, thinking from time to time, 'What a hell of a lot of leaves!' but feeling exactly nothing." There is no poetry without feeling.

Looking through the notebook, I see that I was reading all kinds of poets, many of them Brits—Angela Langfield, Tony Harrison, Charles Tomlinson, Peter Porter—and an American, Anne Winters, who hit me almost as forcefully as Bogan had. I dug deeply into Denise Levertov's work and that of Robert

54

Duncan and Richard Wilbur, before turning to Keats, Shelley, Frost, Lowell, and the other dimly remembered giants from Poetry 101. I read *Endymion* standing in the snow outside an auto-license branch in Jeffersonville, Indiana. I also was finding a Scottish poet, W.S. Graham, who spoke to me about the difficulties of communication, and whose own early poems, some scarcely comprehensible, were like landmines dynamiting the language. And I was studying meter, and making lists of new words, and doing all the things that most "real" poets are doing by their teens. And I was 40! My poor family! What had happened to Daddy?

This is not intended to be a catalog of poetic influences or even a history of how I worked my way through a ton of my own bad writing, gradually figuring out what worked, at least for that poem. As Graham has written: "After one finishes a poem which seems to work one says Ha Ha now I'll write another because I know how to do it but it is not so. There is the silence before one just as difficult to disturb significantly as before."

I ransacked the Louisville Free Public Library and took a very long supper break from the newspaper to hear Richard Wilbur. A friend at the paper, John Filiatreau, had written some fine poems and encouraged me. My first poem was published in 1976 in *Kentucky Poetry Review.* When I left the newspaper in 1979, at least part of the reason was to join an academic community and have more time to write creatively—the extra time turned out to be an illusion.

Eventually I filled a stack of notebooks, had 50-some poems published, most in reputable if not famous magazines, self-published several collections, and had one published by an honest-to-God professional press, not vanity. I got invited to read at the 20th Century Literature Conference of the University of Louisville. In 2005, a 30-year selection was published as *The Landscape Deeper In.* But this is not intended as a record of my successes, and anyway there were far more rejections than acceptances.

What I would rather do is address readers who don't read poetry or think it is only for those with "poetic" imaginations, or is somehow sissified. (Can anyone really think that of such very tough, vivid, *professional* writing?) I think most people are the way I was until age 40. I didn't read poetry much, figured poets lived in some different world from me, didn't know that poetry was my friend next door. Over the years, my wife has read many of my poems and has enjoyed some of them, I think. But she remains convinced that she has no poetic imagination, and this—even if true, which I doubt—is not a crime. I dedicated two collections to her, and the following poem, "To Karen," can stand as the sample of the style I would like to keep always—pretty plain by now; serviceable, I hope, like one of my father's cupboards.

> *I didn't have a poem,*
> *a song, for you,*
> *something your own,*
> *who claim to be*
> *so resolutely unpoetic—*
> *nothing to give you,*
> *no more than the birds have*
> *who take your suet*
> *and thistle, filling*
> *the backyard with their*
> *undedicated songs.*

Do I have any advice for aspiring poets or other writers? Of course. Write if you really want to. If you don't, don't. Pay attention to writers who do it well. Submit your work to editors, don't keep it in the desk drawer. It's good to write regularly, something every day if possible. But I've gone several years without writing much, then come back with a rush. Take criticism for what it's worth, but don't be crushed by it. Early on, a newspaper critic seriously trashed one of my poems and me personally; he would have been quite happy to have stopped me from ever writing another line. Bogan has a few words about losing face and fighting to get it back. If you give up, she says, "the world's insects and worms [will] get up every morning and gargle with Listerine, just as though you had never been." (Am I still sore at the critic? Nah, what gave you that idea?)

Poets tend to worry too much about publication, about fame, about whether what they do is any good. Like most writers, they are perpetually insecure. The best advice is not to worry about things like this. Your job as a writer is to do the very best you can; whether it will live or not isn't up to you— somebody else will decide that. And if trying to be the best is hanging you up, causing writer's block, take poet William Stafford's advice: "Lower your standards." Get back to work. In a poem, "The First Step," by the great Greek poet Cavafy, a sage advises a young poet who has managed only one idyll: "Coming as far as this is not little; what you have achieved is great glory."

A good friend, a self-taught writer (as who isn't?), confessed a while back that she often feels discouraged, wonders if she should be doing this instead of polishing her house to a high gloss, or should sleep at night instead of being up at 3 a.m. struggling with words. She says she can't help herself, which is the test. She has published a children's book, is working on a sequel, goes out and places her books in stores, has sold more copies than I have, and is learning to work with editors and to be a better copyeditor of her own work. Has anyone's tombstone ever read, "She was good at dusting"? To me she is a heroine.

But we need readers, too, so if you're not driven to write, buy a book and make a writer happy. We have this wonderful, crazy language, and it's not the sole property of writers. It belongs to you, too.

Postscript: A few months ago I chased down that first childhood poem in the files of the *Indianapolis News,* to see if it was as good as I remembered. It wasn't; in fact it was pretty punk, even by the kid-poem standard. It will stay buried.

INTERVAL: NEW YORK

In 1973, I was writing from a newspaper conference in New York City to tell Karl, David, and Mike about life in the big city. Some excerpts:

"Manhattan is so big that if you tried to walk from one end to the other it would take all day. So people travel by bus or subway or hop into one of the many hundred taxicabs that cruise the streets all day and night . . . . The subway is a good place to see all the kinds of people who live in, and visit, New York. And since New York is a great international city, every race and country in the world has people living here. Some of them are very new in this country and can't even speak English. People from other countries who want to live in America have always landed in New York first—like Grandpa Fritz's mother and father did when they first came here from Denmark. In the subway you see many blacks, Puerto Ricans, Chinese, beautiful girls with Asian faces, Indians, fat people, thin people, short people, tall people, clean people, dirty people, ones with short hair, long hair, and no hair—all the kinds of people there are in the world, and all New Yorkers.

"New York is full of artists, writers, singers, musicians, actors, actresses, and every other kind of worker. They come because New York has the best theaters, newspapers, magazines, libraries, art galleries, museums, and concerts in the whole country and sometimes in the world. And of course because all of these talented people come, that helps make everything the best. Many young people come because they are good at something and hope that in New York they will be big successes—sometimes they are but sometimes they find they aren't good enough and have to go back home . . . .

"People will tell you sometimes that New Yorkers are cold and unfriendly. This isn't true at all. I'm always stopping them to ask questions or directions and they're almost always happy to answer—if they can. Sometimes it turns out they can't speak English or are in the same boat I am, strangers who also are just visiting New York.

"It's a very interesting and exciting place to be."

58

CHAPTER 10

Four Brothers

Karen has funny blood. She is a rare AB negative, without the Rh factor, and thought for a while as a child that she could never have children. Even when she knew this was not strictly true, it was clear some danger was involved. In the Rh situation, the mother's blood can be incompatible with the child's.

We discussed all this one afternoon in the old wooden swing at her parents' house, and there was no doubt in either of our minds that we wanted kids. With careful pre-natal care and testing, she avoided Rh trouble during three pregnancies, the first with twins, Karl and David. Our advice to all prospective parents: have the twins first. You'll think everybody works this hard, and single babies later will be a snap.

I have my own advice for fathers of twins: forget whatever ideas you may have had about avoiding the messier experiences of child-rearing. Unless you want your wife really to hate you, be prepared to help with the dirtiest jobs and the double loads of bottles and laundry. Someone has described a baby as "an alimentary canal with a loud voice at one end and no responsibility at the other." This is true.

Karl and David were followed after three years by Michael and after nine years more by Colin. They are natives of Indiana, New York, and Kentucky, respectively.

Karen's remark in an earlier chapter about her and the boys playing second fiddle to the newspaper has a certain ring of truth. There seem to be areas of early parenthood that she recalls much better than I do, which leads to the inescapable conclusion that she was there for more of it. But she and they know (I hope) that this did not denote lack of interest or affection on my part. In fact these were great kids, who would have gladdened any father's heart. There wasn't a rotten one in the bunch.

We decided early that we were going to take them everywhere we went, which involved us for some years in tent camping, around Indiana and Kentucky and on a memorable tour of the West.

But the big adventure was Europe. The five of us (Colin hadn't arrived yet) left on the day after Karen's college graduation in 1974 and hit Paris, Venice, Yugoslavia, Germany, and spots in between. Then I had to go back to work, and Karen continued with the boys to her ancestral home in southern Denmark and later to Holland. They were adopted by their Danish hotel and its patrons. Karen was invited to sit at the sacred *stammtisch*, or regulars' table. David got to fish in the neighboring river, and everybody played with Bamsi, a black Newfoundland that has grown larger and shaggier through the years until it is now approaching the proportions of a woolly mammoth.

Our philosophy was simple: travel with the kids while we're all still young. It paid off in Paris when David looked around at a crowded street corner and said, "Mom, we're the foreigners here, aren't we?" There would be fewer ugly Americans if others, including our government, also realized this. A few years later, we made a similar trip with Mike and Colin, and added Greece to the itinerary.

These were four very different youngsters, but they took the brother business seriously. They might scrap among themselves, but it was a united front against the rest of the world. We had a rather old-fashioned household, in which the boys did chores including dishes and were not encouraged to push family democracy too far. One of my frequent lines was "this is a dictatorship and not always a benevolent one." Karen employed "by the time I count to three . . . ." I don't recall that she ever got to three—the consequences were clearly too horrible to contemplate.

As a result, there wasn't much need for corporal punishment. An occasional swat, yes, but colorful threats were usually enough. As I drove through Louisville once, disorder was rampant in the back seat. At the time, escapes were also rampant at the Jefferson County Jail, and a judge had ringed that grim fortress with an electric fence. "We're going to fry 'em like bacon," he said, thus becoming "the bacon-makin' judge."

I pulled up next to the fence and addressed my beloved children: "If you don't cut it out, you're all going (hand extended dramatically toward the bastille) in there!" It got very quiet in the back seat for the rest of the trip.

For a while I was writing down occasional comments and overheard conversations:

Karen (surveying a project): What *is* it?
Karl: Well, maybe it is and maybe it isn't.

Karl, a future librarian, also exclaimed one day, "If this guy Poe is any good, I may give up Nancy Drew."

Colin, a late starter in the brotherly footrace, caught up quickly, and I find him recorded at age 3 during breakfast one morning: "I tell the funny stories, Mike. You don't."

Another conversation, after a snow day at home:

Me (to Colin, age 8): Well, what did you do today?
Colin: Nothing.
Me: Nothing? You must have done something!
Colin: I learned how to spell "disestablishmentarianism." (Mike had spent the snow day doing a little home schooling.)

But my favorite conversation occurred while I was egging Mike on to think of some new holidays. He was taken with my suggestion of Panda Day, but when to celebrate it?

Me: How about today?
Mike: Let's make it tomorrow, so we'll have time to decorate.
Dave (older, jaundiced): You're really weird. What are you going to do—dress up in black and white fur?
Mike: Hey, that's a good idea!

We must have done something right. None of the four is in jail, and the older three are married, to women we like and who have their wits about them. All four are gainfully employed: Karl as a university librarian in Vermont, David as a control-room operator at a nuclear-power plant in Virginia, Mike as a printer tester in Kentucky, and Colin as an actor and writer in New York City. They keep in touch with each other and call home often to make sure their doddering parents haven't skidded off the rails.

In fact one of them called as I was writing the paragraph above. As he talked with Karen and me, I asked innocently if he knew that the word "gullible" wasn't in the dictionary. "I have a dictionary right here," he replied. "Aren't you impressed?" Sound of pages turning. Sound of parents losing it. "Caught another one, Ma!"

From left: Michael, Colin, Karl, and David.

CHAPTER 11

A Funny Little Place

I became a college professor in 1979 after teaching exactly one course—half-teaching it, actually, since I teamed with a real professor, who did most of the work. We told graduate social-work students how to woo the news media, and my colleague later wrote a paper about it, which we were invited to deliver to a national meeting in Los Angeles. When we arrived, we found this meant sitting at a table and handing out copies. My old newspaper boss thought it was hilarious. "You delivered papers!" he cackled. "You were a paper boy!"

My lack of academic credentials was no problem at Franklin, which was even more desperate than Harvey Jacobs had suggested. Two of its three journalism teachers had left more than a year before. Some of the 29 journalism students were being bused to nearby cities for classes taught by alumni. Anything I did would be an improvement. Suddenly the gag headline about the college closing didn't seem so funny. Enrollment was skidding toward 500, maintenance had been neglected for decades, and the ramshackle tower of Old Main recalled the TV series *Dark Shadows*. In winter, snow blew through cracks into classrooms and offices. The place looked much as it had when I graduated in 1956—"this funny little place," one new colleague called it, with affection.

As the dean and I finished our salary discussion (I had talked him into an extra $100 a year so I could say my income had risen), he said, "Oh, by the way, you can be journalism department chair if you want." Sure, why not? It was just one more thing I didn't know how to do.

But I had a profound sense of being home. On a spring day, I stood in the Webster debate hall with its ancient green carpet and looked out at redbud blossoming beside the stone benches given by the class of 1915. In its decay, the campus seemed immemorial, a piece of my own past frozen in time, where my mother was teaching when I was born. I used my new faculty powers to look up my father's grades from 1927. "I think we should talk about your 'C' in sociology," I told him. "How did you find out about that?" he sputtered. "Are there no privacy laws? Is there no statute of limitations?"

What Franklin still had, besides nostalgia, was a hard-working faculty and staff, some dedicated alums and trustees, and a faith that the doors would stay open somehow. And there were the students—kids from central Indiana, mostly, who were often the first in their families to attend college. They didn't know campuses were supposed to be bright and shiny, with dorm rooms like deluxe hotel suites.

Once more, Karen signed a peace treaty with my job and came aboard as unpaid secretary and den mother for journalism students. I helped hire a young copyeditor from Milwaukee, Rich Gotshall, to round out our three-member faculty. (The third was due to retire in a year.) Rich and I agreed that we could do anything that no one had specifically forbidden—"ask forgiveness, not permission." We were in business.

In long hindsight, I can see this was a job I badly needed. It could absorb any amount of energy, obsession, and do-good impulses. Unlike the rest of the college, journalism had some dedicated funds that no one had figured out how to spend. Could I spend other people's money? Yes, I believed I could. Rich and I organized conferences, brought in speakers, beat the drums for journalism and the rest of the college, even taught classes—four a semester for me and three for Rich, who was also running the Indiana High School Press Association out of his hip pocket. We showed up at a student costume party—I was a pencil with a pointy hat and a yellow stripe down my back that said "Eberhard Faber #2." We had one shining credential—we were fresh from the real world and knew people who had jobs and internships to offer.

We brought in Sam Day, editor of the *Progressive* magazine, which had just published a controversial account of how to build an H-bomb. And Walter Sullivan, science editor of the *New York Times.* "You have a phone call," someone told me. "Tell 'em I'll call back later," I replied. When Sullivan arrived, he remarked, "Usually when I tell people it's the *New York Times* calling, they come to the phone."

Another *NYT* staffer, formerly of Louisville, addressed a reporting class. Partway through her talk, the class and I saw one of the building's giant cockroaches crawling up the wall behind her. I tore off a shoe, ran forward, and smashed it, to the cheers of the students. Another class researched small-city newspapers and decided that the country's best was the *News-Chronicle* of Thousand Oaks, Calif. A friend and I called on its bemused editor, Marvin Sosna, and invited him to campus for a week. "I thought at first you were spies from the *L.A. Times,* out to steal my secrets," he said later. We also joined forces with the English department to bring in poets and other good writers (my own poetry had gone into a drawer for the time being).

We two hotshots would not have lasted long, though, had not the faculty wrapped its arms around us. "This funny little place" had teachers who knew their subjects, their students, and each other. Dick Graham from English took me to my first academic conference. He also was watching one day as I hurried across campus, turned back for something, then changed my mind and resumed course. "Congratulations, Bill," he said. "You're already going in two directions at once. If you learn to go in circles, you can be a dean."

I was journalism chair for 10 years, during which a lot happened. The college didn't close, but in 1985 two fires, both accidental, destroyed 40 per cent of its residential, classroom, and office space. A new president and the trustees raised money and rebuilt the campus into a showplace. The president claimed that at conferences colleagues took him aside to ask the name of his arsonist. I had a similar experience. Karen called me at a meeting in Texas to say that a burglar had stolen all the department's decrepit manual typewriters. My fellow conference-goers were intrigued. "If you catch the guy, could you send him to my school?" one asked.

During reconstruction, we learned to love bulldozers or at least live with them. Professors and administrators shared space, in trailers and sometimes in "offices" separated only by tape on the floor. It was a great bonding experience. "I want to stay here," one professor said, "until they call me Old Lady _____ and carry me out the door." People kept their sense of humor. On the morning after the first fire, a directional sign appeared on the mall next to the smouldering ruins. "Smoking Section," said one arrow; "Non-Smoking Section" said the other. Strangely, the fires and the uproar led to the college's virtual rebirth. It was all publicity. The president talked so much about the phoenix rising from the ashes that we half-expected it to appear on the cafeteria menu for Thanksgiving.

There were battles—UPI's Dieter Schmidt had some worthy successors among VPs for finance. Soon after my arrival, journalism students uncovered a messy story about a local businessman who was also a donor to the college. I was summoned to Old Main, where the president of that time and the untenured professor sparred for an hour. Then he let me go. "Try not to do it again," he said, "or I may have to break your legs."

I found that teaching was tough, gritty work; good teachers earn their summer holidays, which they often spend preparing for the fall and doing the scholarly work there's no time for once classes start. When I left the newspaper, my colleagues thought I had retired, but I was working harder than ever. Among the first revelations: teaching is an entirely different profession from journalism. The neophyte can get by on experience and war stories for about a year. By then he had better know some things about public speaking, motivating students, and making course plans, or syllabi. (I asked the dean, whimsically, why two syllabuses were syllabi, but two school buses were not school bi. He launched into an explanation of Latin plurals; I was definitely in academia.)

Over the years, calls came now and then from aging former colleagues looking for a quiet pasture, and I had to disillu-
sion them. One called just as the 5 p.m. college chimes were
sounding. "Ah, I can see it now," he exclaimed. "The bells
from the old tower, the ivy-covered walls . . . ." "Cool it,
John," I told him. "The bells are recorded and the tower is falling down." "And I suppose the ivy is fake, too," he said.

In the aftermath of fires and reconstruction, the college
grew to more than 1,000 students, and journalism grew along
with it. We got our own building, and later a lot of money
when newspaper stock owned by the college turned out to be
worth millions. But after 10 years I had worn down. Keeping
tabs one week, I found that I had worked 80 hours, my UPI
maximum, and I was 30 years older. A new chair took over and
I cut back to teaching, committee work, and advising the student paper. I made a trip to Taiwan as a guest of the government, and did a workshop with the staff of its weekly English-
language newspaper, the *Free China Journal*, and the paper's
editor, Carol Cho.

Back home, a faculty-administration war was on, and
some things about my job had soured. The clock was running
again, and I began sending resumés to interesting places: the
Poynter journalism institute in Florida; the American University of Bulgaria; the University of the Solomon Islands, which
wanted a distance-learning director over a large swath of the
Pacific; and National Taiwan University for which I got a recommendation from Carol Cho. Rejections dribbled in. Then
one Saturday morning in April, 1993, as Karen and I lingered
over breakfast, the phone rang. It was Carol in Taiwan. How
would I like to be senior copyeditor of the *Free China Journal*?
I was already scheduled for a summer faculty internship with
the Scripps Howard News Service in Washington, D.C., but I
could go directly from there to Taipei. It was a chance to make
a million dollars a year, even though these were New Taiwan
Dollars worth about six cents each.

Karen and I had a long talk. This might be a permanent
move to Asia, and she would have to stay behind for a year
while Colin finished high school. "Go for it," she said. The
dean agreed with suspicious swiftness to a year's leave of ab-

sence, and I was on my way to the Orient by way of the Potomac. "To go a mile west, go a mile east," says a Zen *koan*.

The Taiwan job turned out not to be permanent, but it reset the job clock. I came back to Franklin refreshed, writing poetry again, and ready to stay until retirement, although this was delayed two years so I could create a new post of journalism director. The next permanent director was one of my students from 1979. Somewhere, Harvey Jacobs was surely smiling.

The college when I left in 2003 was much different than it had been nearly a quarter of a century before—and a world away from the still funnier little place of my student years. It was bigger, glossier, more efficient. Higher priced, too. Students and parents had learned to demand those shiny buildings and deluxe dorm rooms. It was probably better educationally, though this is harder to measure. Who can tell what book, what casual remark, what friendship has changed a life in ways forever beyond the reach of outcomes-based assessment?

Near the end of my stay in academia, I had also been the college's director of Canadian Studies—others had the Canadian expertise, I knew how to organize and promote. One day I found that the business office had shortchanged Canadian Studies by $87.14. The budget year was over and the books closed; the error couldn't be fixed by anyone less than the vice president for finance. I had learned a few things by now about academic battles, and also knew that the VP, though a money man, had a sense of humor. So I prepared a dossier, with appendices, explaining the error and giving a timeline on how it had happened. There were indices, tabs, and supporting documents, with a cover letter warning of trouble to come with the Canadian government. The letter concluded, "I had planned to retire this year, but have decided to remain indefinitely until this matter is resolved."

The VP responded instantly: "I have restored $87.14 to the Canadian Studies account. If you will take early retirement, I'll double it."

CHAPTER 12

'My Horse Was Sick'

No student ever told me that a dog ate his term paper. The closest was a woman who missed class because "my horse was sick." And I knew it was absolutely true; she was a farm wife going to school part time, and it was the only class she missed all semester. I tried to find a get-well card for a horse, but this was one possibility Hallmark had overlooked.

In 24 years as a professor at a small college, I taught at most 3,000 students, not factoring in those who took more than one class from me or who flunked and were trying again. It was nowhere near the record of a grad school professor of mine, who told me years later that he was about to teach the 10,000[th] student in his signature and incredibly boring class. What a thing to have on your conscience, I thought.

Of those 3,000 students, I can vaguely recognize most of the names. But even good students fade from memory unless they were outstanding, go on to fame and fortune, or have kept in touch after graduation. On the other hand, we remember our problem children forever.

Among those memorable in a good way was Connie, who needed a January internship in the early 1980s. She wanted to go to the East Coast and write about animals, which immediately suggested the Bronx Zoo. My Uncle Bill had retired as the zoo's curator of publications, and a call to his successor got

Connie on board at *Animal Kingdom* magazine. But how to keep her afloat in the big city?

More phone calls produced free lodging: a week in a zoo apartment, a week at Bill's (with the loan of his car), and two weeks as a Manhattan apartment sitter for a *New York Times* staffer—the same one I had saved from the giant cockroach. But Connie still had no food or walking-around money, so I launched a discreet but worldwide fund drive. Some 50 fliers went out to friends and fellow journalists, with a photo of Connie looking waiflike. "Send Connie to New York!" the headline urged. "Help this Hoosier girl, who's never even been on an airplane, have the experience of her life." Some $500 came in, more than enough spending money for that era. John Callcott contributed from Geneva, and Walter Sullivan of the *New York Times* sent a check. "I'm not sure what sort of scam you're running," a friend wrote, "but you should know that I have recorded the serial numbers of my bills."

The internship went smoothly until near the end, when Connie's mother called frantically one night after being unable to reach her daughter for three evenings straight at the Manhattan apartment. I phoned a New York contact who had a boyfriend in the NYPD. Then I called Connie's best friend, Carolyn, who began laughing. "Well, you see, she met this guy from Canada . . . ." When the Canadian returned Connie to the apartment after midnight, one of New York's Finest was waiting to tell her to call Mom.

Another student had a January internship in Indianapolis, but no transportation. I loaned her a ponderous 1965 Ford Fairlane inherited from Karen's mother, but it shed its entire exhaust system the first day as she turned onto the interstate. The college finally coughed up a car.

And there was Rachel Sheeley, who needed an internship north of the border to get her Canadian Studies minor. Rachel was already noted for winning the national Bulwer-Lytton contest for the worst opening to a novel. Her grand-prize effort:

> *Like an expensive sports car, fine-tuned and well-built,*
> *Portia was sleek, shapely, and gorgeous, her red*
> *jumpsuit molding her body, which was as warm as the*

seat covers in July, her hair as dark as new tires, her eyes flashing like bright hubcaps, and her lips as dewy as fresh rain on the hood; she was a woman driven— fueled by a single accelerant—and she needed a man, a man who wouldn't shift from his views, a man to steer her along the right road, a man like Alf Romeo.

Anyone who could write that wretchedly had to be very good. I called a contact at the Yukon Archives in Whitehorse, where I had done some research, and pitched Rachel as an intern. "You were here in July, Bill," the archivist said. "Do you realize how cold it gets in January?" I assured her that Rachel was as tough as they came, but the internship never jelled. Rachel ended up at the *Brandon Sun* in Manitoba, where she had a great time and learned curling.

Alas, some other students were memorable for the wrong reasons. One was Jeremy, whom I encountered after being drafted to teach remedial writing for the English department. He was gangling and red-haired, with an attitude even taller than he was. He read ostentatiously from a newspaper as I lectured. His first assigned theme, on "something I'm an expert at," was titled "Procrastination," and it came in three weeks late. "Good theme," I told him, "but don't try to live out your philosophy in this class."

We kept butting heads. I warned a visiting speaker about him, and she asked him a question, which he didn't deign to answer. But later he said, "She scared me. She knew my name." One day he left his chair and lay down on the floor, until I asked if he would like me to call the campus nurse (or the campus police, I was thinking). But things began to change. He actually wrote well and somehow we reached an accord. He stopped acting out and passed the class. I never expected to see him again, but we met on campus the next fall and without a word shook hands and went our ways. He later joined the military, which was probably good for him, although I'm not so sure it was for national defense.

Early in my teaching career—when PDA meant "public display of affection"—a young couple sat in the front row of my reporting class one morning, holding hands. "Isn't young love sweet?" I thought to myself. A few minutes later, he had his arm around her shoulder and she was cuddling against him. "Hmmmm," I thought. Just before the bell, the cuddle turned into a full-scale clinch, and I stopped the boy on his way out to suggest that they restrain themselves a bit. He broke out laughing and said, "We're doing an experiment for Professor X in sociology, to see just how far professors will let us go." I'm still not sure how far that would have been, but I'm glad it was a 50-minute class and not an hour-long one.

Then there was Rocky, who was hard to categorize—nice guy, no great student, but he once gave me an important piece of information. "If you swim in Florida," he said, "it's okay to go out as far as the second sandbar. Sharks don't come up past the second sandbar." Words to live by—I hope. One student took her journalism degree and became a go-go dancer. One (male) wore a dress and wrote like a dream. And more than one became first-rate professional reporters or editors.

But there were also some troubling cases. A student legislative intern interviewed a state senator, who didn't like what she wrote and threatened her with disgrace if she didn't get the story killed. Despite her tearful pleas, the school paper ran her story, and then suddenly the senator was all smiles and apologies. Politicians!

During the fires of the '80s, student reporters worked all night, put out special fire editions, and wrote dozens of good stories that helped rally the campus. Student journalists never win Pulitzer Prizes, but I nominated them for one anyway; it was the only way to adequately compliment them for their good work and professionalism.

Another newspaper staff, celebrating after a tough edition, brought beer into the newsroom in violation of college policy. Then they took pictures of themselves drinking, which someone delivered to the dean of students. There were penalties for all, and the students made their own sins the lead story in the next edition. Truth in journalism!

At a small college, professors deal with the personal problems of students almost as much as with the academic ones. Sometimes the problem is both. I called in a student after she had missed several of my classes. "I'm missing *all* my classes," she said. "I don't know why, and it's scary. I get halfway there, can't go any further, and go back to my room." We decided she had "classophobia," and I told her, "We'll talk for a while, and when I get up to go to class, just walk along with me. You'll be okay." She was amused, and that was the end of her hitherto unknown, but genuine, ailment.

A wonderful thing about students is that they haven't learned yet what they can't do. Two male students decided to drive to Colorado and meet their literary idol, the gonzo journalist Hunter Thompson. They tracked him at night up the lonely road to his house, which (if I recall correctly) was guarded by gateposts with skulls. They knocked; Thompson came to the door and talked with them for a minute or two before advising that it would be dangerous for them to stay on his property. The students couldn't have been happier.

Right after 9/11, a carload of student reporters took off for New York. "They won't get within a mile of Ground Zero," I thought. They not only did, but also joined an aid station and got a front-page story and photos for their next edition.

Closer to home, reporters Steve and Andy grabbed cameras and headed off to cover a tornado in the northern part of the county. They filmed lots of damage and a dead pig, which they delighted in putting on the front page of the paper. A journalistic first!

It must have been soon after this that Steve wrote a memo explaining how much better a job he could do of running the journalism school than the faculty was doing. Not to be out-memoed, I sent my own to a colleague with a leaked copy to Steve.

"I'm taking a big chance sending you this without routing it through Steve," I wrote, "but I think you'll agree that he has finally gone too far . . . . I've arranged to have him removed to the fourth floor of Old Main, where he'll join the earlier newspaper editors who had too much fun on the job. (There are no yearbook editors—they never have any fun.) I applaud your suggestion of building an exact replica of the student newsroom over there; with luck, Steve will continue to believe that he's in college and putting out the paper. Poor soul—we must do what we can."

I still see Steve now and then, and when he found I was writing this memoir, he asked how up to date it would be. "Up to about 20 seconds ago," I said. "Listen up, everybody," he shouted. "Stop talking to him. Right now!"

You can see why, when I began pondering a move to the *Free China Journal* in Taiwan, a big regret was leaving students behind. But I needn't have worried—as it turned out, I was simply trading Smiths and Browns, Rachels and Steves, for other young journalists named Yu, Pun, Chiu, Lin, and Shen. Teaching went right ahead.

'Twas Halloween in the newsroom: Editor-in-chief Jennifer Prall and the adviser in the office of the college student newspaper, *The Franklin.*

CHAPTER 13

A Very Personal Year

On the night of August 3, 1993, I was in the Taipei YMCA, wondering if I had just made the worst mistake of my life. I was 58 years old. Beyond my window was a vast Asiatic city, with crowds milling through dimly-lit streets. It looked like a set from *Batman.* Everyone I knew and loved was 8,000 miles away. What was I doing here?

The next morning, at my new desk in the Government Information Office, a letter was waiting from a favorite correspondent. I was welcomed by Carol Cho, by the staff I had met the previous summer, and by Sam Dixon, my American co-editor on the *Free China Journal.* Perhaps this would work after all. But the question of what I was doing remained. There were pat answers—curiosity, flight from routine, the mountain-climber's reply. But of the real reasons, I knew as little as my father did in the 1930s when he changed his salary into gold "double eagles" each payday before converting it again into spending currency. I had been invited, I had come.

Let me go back a few months. When I had visited Taipei in 1992, it was as a VIP guest, part of a government program to woo foreign journalists. I lived and dined at the sumptuous Lai-Lai Sheraton; Chinese soldiers snapped off salutes as my chauffeured car rolled by. "I could get used to this," I told Karen later. "Forget it. You're home now," she said.

I had, in fact, done some work on that trip, interviewing officials and journalists, and writing newspaper columns. I had spent a week on my own in the coastal city of Hualien, reading and thinking (and in a bizarre moment being pursued through the streets by a demented woman who mistook me for a Christian missionary). I loved Taiwan—what an interesting place, what energy! I wanted to go back.

The road back, a year later, had begun with Carol Cho's invitation and led through Washington, D.C., where I worked 10 weeks for the Scripps Howard News Service and lived in a rooming house near Dupont Circle. I had sublet a tiny six-sided room, with a huge Communist Chinese flag hanging over the futon—odd in light of my eventual destination.

It was a fun summer, with sociable housemates, an art gallery nearby, and interesting news work. Karen and I met in Virginia for the late-June wedding of our son David to Connie Godwin, and Karen returned later to put me on the plane to Taipei. "Goodbye, love," she said softly at the gate—words I was clinging to a few hours later in the YMCA.

My first Taipei friend was Sam Dixon, who took me to lunch that first day. On the way, one of the few birds to survive Taipei's air pollution dumped on my shirt. Sam pulled me into a shop, bought tissues and a bottle of water, and cleaned me up. I didn't know it then, but that quick act of kindness would be typical of life in Taipei. The year soon became a very personal one, in which friends played more of a part than my job or even the exotic surroundings. This was unexpected. I don't know quite what I *had* expected. Just another job probably, like UPI/Germany but with more time for sightseeing. It did not turn out that way at all.

The job was easy. Expectations for our little newspaper were modest, and the office was well-staffed. The overachieving new editor had to review his role—and was strangely relieved. For the first time in memory, I could set a moderate pace, go home at five, and forget work until the next morning. I did some sightseeing, getting up at 4 a.m. to watch the celebration of Confucius's 2,543rd birthday—Teachers' Day in China. Karen got an account of the fake sacrificial animals, the students in gold and purple robes with ostrich plumes, the "literary and martial dances," and a cool breeze that swept the hot and crowded temple just as the "spirit of the Sage" departed. I also visited the Lin An-t'ai Homestead, where a dozen bridal parties were being photographed against the antique dwellings.

But Taipei is not famed for its sights. Its attraction is its life as a city, its thousands of shops and restaurants, its back lanes, and small surprises. Walking down one of the lanes, I passed a man carefully arranging dozens of firecrackers on a garden wall. "He's going to set those off all at once," I thought, and before I had gone 50 feet he did.

Taipei that year was building a subway and characteristically was doing it not in stages but all at once. Streets were torn up everywhere, pushing the manic tide of traffic onto the sidewalks. Now and then "ghost trains"—test cars—went by on the elevated Mucha line. It was said that cracks had been found in the line's support pillars and that the problem would be addressed by hiding the cracks with ivy. In Taipei, this sounded possible. A car with a Chinese family fell into a four-story subway excavation—everyone emerged unhurt. At a surging intersection, I watched nervously as a father pushed his little son, school bag on back, into the traffic. The child, a born Taipeier, sailed through the swarm more easily than I did.

"The Chinese have a tremendous tolerance for disorder," a friend said. Then he laughed. "Of course just saying 'disorder' betrays the western mindset—to the Chinese, it's just their form of order." I saw it a little more simply—Taipei was the antithesis of Indianapolis.

In that very personal year, one of the chief persons was Sam, an expatriate in his late 30s and an ardent wooer of Chinese ballerinas with names like Tulip. He was the only man I knew who sewed his tie to his shirt each morning rather than use a tie bar. He was also a poet and the author of an unpublished cult classic, *Outer Begonia*, about life in Taiwan. I got to know its first line, "Drizzle becomes rain," quite well, because whenever Sam finished a chapter he would read the entire novel to us from the beginning. He was a good friend, and together we made sure the *Free China Journal's* English was impeccable.

My first few days were a blur of logistics problems, from getting an "alien registration card" to finding somewhere to live. I was taken to an apartment where I would have shared living arrangements with "Sylvia." This did not seem like a good idea. Jessica Chen, a co-worker at the *Free China Journal,* finally rented me her parents' western-style apartment at the top of a 14-story building at the intersection of Chunghsiao East and Chienkuo South roads. The apartment overlooked Taipei and the mountains beyond; the Taipei flower and jade markets were nearby. I might have gotten deeper into Chinese culture by living in a low-rent suburban warren, but I couldn't have coped with that much strangeness. From my building it was a half-hour walk to work along Chunghsiao, and on the way I could press my nose against the glass of the Lai-Lai Sheraton breakfast room, where I had eaten as a VIP a year before.

Turning right from the Lai-Lai each morning, I reached the GIO, punched a time clock, and climbed to the newspaper's second-floor office. Down the hall, in the *Taiwan Yearbook* office, were Jon Welch, Fred Steiner, and Mary Tzen, who invited me to learn bridge with them during the daily hour-and-a-half lunch breaks. They also had a coffee pot. It was just 100 paces from my office to theirs, and they urged me to think of the "100-step snake," whose venom kills its victims within that distance unless an antidote (coffee in this case) can be administered.

Fred, a formidable intellect, was fluent in Mandarin and Taiwanese, and was learning Cantonese. He also had a pixie sense of humor. Phoning him one day with a computer problem, I asked, "Is this Mr. Science?" "Yes," he replied, "and you will remember, children, that yesterday we built a chicken."

Jon was a young writer/translator who knew no distinctions of age. He became my closest friend in Taipei, ferrying me around the city to bookstores and restaurants on the back of his motorscooter. We ate a lot of *ai-yu,* a shaved-ice concoction, in the Liaoning Street night market. I became a fan of ai-kido, the defensive martial art, when Jon and a Chinese teammate won their class in Taiwan national competition.

Mary was the Coffee Queen. She said her hand began shaking one day as she poured, and she thought, "I've got to cut out the caffeine." Then she realized it was an earthquake.

An old China hand, Bob Irick, sometimes joined us for bridge; he lived near me and we went out to neighborhood eating places like the Yellow River Fish Restaurant and the Cat's Stomach. He dared me one night to order chicken feet, which are tasty if you can forget that they look like tiny human hands. Being well-connected, Bob also got free tickets for the two of us to everything from Finnish folk dancers to the New York Philharmonic.

There were other subgroups of the English-speaking community. One, drawn from various agencies and businesses, went out once a month to eat, bar hop, and comment profanely on Taiwan and the Chinese. Privately, I called them "the Cynical Journalists," but they were welcoming and I became a regular. One night in the Mariner Bar, I watched them romance a complaisant bar girl, then saw the same girl later as she hauled sacks of garbage to the curb. All in a night's work. I spent one evening with the American staff of the *China Post* in the Dinosaur Bar, a four-story beer hall featuring a giant plastic T. Rex skeleton on the roof. (The *Post* housed its employees in its own dormitory where, the editor said, "my shower curtain has more biodiversity than a South American rain forest.")

There were also meetings of "Grey Dawn Breaking," its name taken from a John Masefield poem. It consisted of Jon Welch, Sam Dixon, France Yu (a Chinese colleague), and me, and met at our apartments to drink beer and recite poetry, usually in that order. France captivated me with one of her lines: "The Yangtse River stops at my feet." I also met Mike O'Connor, a fine poet, and we went to coffee shops and the Ancient Rain Café to exchange poems and talk about writing. I went to Chinese weddings and joined a Chinese church—more about that later.

The heavy contact with English speakers, at work and afterward, made it harder to learn Chinese, but I persisted with the lessons begun in Washington at Wang's Chinese Boxing Association and Language School. And I kept the name—Bei Hau-wen—that my teacher there had given me. He said it meant "Mr. Great Knowledge," and I grew so fond of explaining this that a friend finally said, "You know, Bill, it can also be translated as 'Mr. Know-It-All.'"

There were many personal moments, at work and elsewhere, with Chinese who spoke English to some degree. During a newspaper luncheon, I queried my Chinese tablemate about the small roasted fowls we were eating:

Me: This certainly is delicious. What kind of bird is it?
Miss Chiu: Oh, it is a very lovely bird!
Me: I hope it's not a nightingale, or some other endangered species.
Miss Chiu: Oh, no! It is a bird that begins with a D—it has something to do with peace.
Me: My God! I've just eaten the Dove of Peace!"

Editing a Chinese newspaper—a weekly government one for distribution to libraries and scholars abroad—was different from journalism American-style. Despite the unfailing courtesy of the Chinese, it was clearly their newspaper and their country. Although hired as a native speaker of English, I had to justify editing decisions to my co-workers and to Mr. Chen, the superior entrusted with the oversight of English usage in GIO publications. When Bruce Babbitt, the U.S. secretary of the interior, visited Taiwan, the Chinese editors insisted on spelling his name "Babbit." "Your own government spells it that way!" one cried, waving a misspelled press release from a U.S. agency. It took several other printed sources, including *Time* magazine, to persuade them.

But such battles were rare. Respect and courtesy worked as well in Taipei as anywhere else, and sometimes better. Most of the staffers wrote and spoke fairly competent English; Sam and I could help them out on finer points. They became good friends, and even Mr. Chen unbent occasionally. He was amazed when I coined a word, "boatel," to describe a floating dormitory. "Are you allowed to do that in English?" he asked.

The *Free China Journal* was an eight-page tabloid, reasonably free of propaganda, although it tended toward features and "soft" coverage of the government and the ruling Kuomintang. There was no hard-hitting investigative reporting. Irritated once by an official car that blocked my bus stop, I asked a reporter with police contacts to check out the license number.

He declined politely; the police would ask why we wanted to know, he said. I was living illegally in my apartment, since the owner wasn't paying the lodgings tax; it occurred to me that perhaps I didn't want to invite police questions either.

Our reporters wrote in English, and several had graduated from U.S. journalism schools. But confronted with a translation difficulty, they went to their Chinese-English dictionaries and selected words not actually used in English since the 18th Century. I had to go to the dictionary myself to find that a "cadastral survey" was simply one of land ownership. I also learned to be careful with criticism after a reporter was fired, in part because the American editor had taken issue with her story. I only wanted her to go back and ask more questions!

An unexpected benefit of the Taipei year was the strength of the support system for Karen and me. Letters came from friends, relatives, former students, even my old professor, Harvey Jacobs, who took Karen out to a classy restaurant. ("Your wife was seen having an inanimate lunch at the Manor," a friend wrote hastily. "Inanimate is fine," I replied.)

Our sons checked in frequently with their mother and came home for a big Christmas. They also wrote and called me, and Mike began a chess-by-mail game that went on for eight years. Karen's friend, Sheron Miller, helped her laugh through the bleaker days, and was rewarded with a pair of brass dragons, named Frick and Frack, for the two girl friends. At some point, I realized that all these relationships were what I would value most from the year—and that I never again wanted to be trapped in stale routine or campus warfare.

The most personal part of the year was, of course, with Karen. We were spending our first substantial time apart in more than 30 years of a close marriage. In many ways, she had the toughest part of the adventure—looking after the Franklin household and seeing our son Colin through his last year of high school (and then sending him off alone for a summer as a theater apprentice in Seattle). She rarely complained, although she did say at one point, "I didn't get married to live with a teenager and four cats." (But she added, "Colin is a great guy, and I've told him so.") We ran up huge phone bills, and wrote

81

several hundred letters, from love notes to reports on a flooded basement and a chronically ailing car.

Only once, in January, 1994, was the marriage severely tested. On the phone one Sunday, I complained about freezing without central heating in a 55-degree cold snap. "That's about 90 degrees warmer than it is here," Karen replied, with a bit of a cold snap herself. The previous night's low had been 36 degrees below zero, breaking all Indiana records. Pipes were frozen and the driveway was clogged with snow. A veteran husband, I arranged for the delivery of a green plant, and then the florist gave her hell for not having the driveway shoveled.

But we soon were on the downhill side of the year. Karen came to Taipei for a month in February, and my letter just before takeoff left no doubt of my feelings. "Be aboard!" I wrote. "Do not worry if not everything gets done before you leave. Come directly to Taipei, do not pass Go. Come in your shimmy-shirt if you have to, but come!"

During her visit, we talked about whether to make a permanent move. She liked the city and picked up taxi-driver Chinese quickly. But I was chafing at some aspects of the job—there wasn't enough real work to do! Also, the group of friends and colleagues who had made the year a delight was starting to break up. Carol Cho had gone, and with her a certain commitment to change and to improving the paper. I was starting to miss my students at home, and we were both thinking about being half a world away from our sons and any future grandchildren.

We had a wonderful Valentine's Day. A Chinese girl walking with her date turned and gave her own red rose to Karen. But in the end we decided not to become expatriates. I gave notice to the paper at the end of May, and later went through a typhoon and a mild but quite sufficient earthquake. (A ceiling fell on Sam and his Tulip of the moment, sending them to a hotel.) In early September, after a farewell luncheon and a karaoke party, I flew home.

"I'm glad we did it," Karen said, "and we're never going to do it again—unless it's together."

CHAPTER 14

A Tree in Taipei

I was homesick for Taipei. Something had happened there that I couldn't quite identify. I thought of Auden's words: "Somewhere are places where we have really been, dear spaces / of our deeds and faces . . . ."

When the chance came to return for a few days in the spring of 1996, I took it. A group was forming to observe, unofficially, Taiwan's first direct presidential election. I lined up a newspaper client or two, got some financial help from the college, and on a steamy May night found myself back in the Taipei YMCA—but unstressed this time. Word had been relayed that Jessica Chen, my former landlady, could get me a room for practically nothing at the Hilton; all I had to do was to identify myself to the proper person as "Mr. Chen." Thinking of my nearly total lack of resemblance to anyone named Chen, I stuck with the Y.

I had several reasons to return to Taipei. One was to renew acquaintances at Ling Leung Church, especially with Linda Yew. Explaining this requires going back in some detail to the low point of my earlier year in Taipei. It was October, 1993, a bad month. I was lonely and a little sick. One day I felt the onset of a panic attack. Taking a deep breath, I went home and called Jon Welch: "Let's go to the night market and eat *ai-yu*,"

I said. Jon proposed instead that we have supper at his apartment with his fiancée, Jun-yi. We ate, talked about ordinary things, and my anxiety passed.

But I had had a warning. My imagination is too vivid—without people around whom I know and love it can lead me quickly into depression. Hell is a country where you are entirely by yourself, locked up in your own mind. I had been there as a college student and didn't want to go back.

Earlier in that same October week, I was crossing a busy intersection when I heard a voice call, "Professor Bridges!" No one knew me in Taipei as a professor. What was going on?

The caller was Lucky Koo, a former Franklin student, who was in Taipei only for that day and happened to be passing the intersection just as I was. How coincidental. We went out for supper, and he put me in touch with the English-speaking congregation at Ling Leung Church, who became my family through the rest of my year in Taipei. I went to "home group" with them, tagged along on trips outside Taipei, and played a rather tall and skinny Santa Claus in a Christmas fête. Mary Tzen turned out to be a member, as did Linda Yew, a remarkable freelance missionary. Linda told how she had been abused as a child, had forgiven her abusers, and been led to care for the most desperately needy of Taipei, including Filipina housemaids held in virtual bondage by their employers.

The multinational and mostly young Christians of Ling Leung also persuaded me to stop agonizing about faith and simply accept it as an amazing and inexplicable gift. No, reader, this is not a Damascus Road experience or an attempt at conversion. It is a Chunghsiao Road experience, which is where I was when I finally gave up and said, "I will never understand this, but I am going to accept it once and for all"—or "to the absolute bloody end!" as the writer Sean O'Faolain describes a similar moment. O'Faolain acknowledged that his experience would not be the same for readers, and neither will mine. I simply record it here.

I began to get a handle in Taipei on whatever it was that had driven me for years to work harder, stay up later, do more than anybody else. (At a New York newspaper conference once, a roomful of my cohorts talked idly about jetting to London for the weekend. They weren't serious; I slipped out and priced tickets.)

Perhaps part of the change was the slowing of the machinery, but some was just the blesséd realization that I didn't have to do everything. I could spend a day loafing on Yangmingshan mountain or bake bread in the toaster oven that Karen had lugged across the Pacific. I was no longer proving something, what a relief.

Fast forward again a couple of years to Taipei in 1996. I toured polling places on election day, and saw President Lee Teng-hui win another term. From a phone booth at the YMCA, I dictated stories back to Karen for the newspapers. Then I revisited scenes from two years earlier. The streets were still torn up for the subway, but the Mucha line was finished and I rode for free during its opening week. I stopped at Bob Irick's apartment, where he loaned me a typewriter to do a story. Bob and I had kept in regular touch, and now we went out one more time to the Yellow River Fish Restaurant. Bob died several years later, but not before I fulfilled one request from this old Missourian; I bought out my local supermarket's stock of Quick Quaker Grits and shipped half a dozen boxes to him.

Jon and Jun-yi had married and moved to the U.S., but I met Fred Steiner in Keelong, near which the mainland Chinese had been firing practice missiles in an effort to influence the election. Fred and I did man-on-the-street interviews in the Keelong night market, with Fred asking questions and translating the answers for me. Then we went to his apartment to fire off a story to the States, using his e-mail connection this time.

On Sunday I went to church at Ling Leung. Mary Tzen was there with her husband, John Ho, and their baby. I thought back two years, and remembered her questioning me earnestly as she considered marriage. With absolutely no experience in advising daughters, I gave her the tritest of answers—but it had all worked out. After church, we had lunch with Linda Yew and caught up with her ministry. She also told me how she had once left a religious group that had turned into a cult. Linda was a thinking Christian as well as (and how she would hate my saying this) one of the most shining souls I have ever met.

FIVE-MOUNTAIN MORNING

Sometime during those spring days of 1996, I also visited the *Free China Journal*, where the staff took me to lunch. A few people had left, but many of those I remembered were still there. We had a happy two hours—stretching even the leisurely lunch break—before scattering again.

Later that day—a rainy afternoon—the bus I was riding passed my old apartment building and the courtyard with its familiar tree. The tree was real, not a memory—I could have jumped off the bus and touched it. But two years had passed. There was a distance now, and a veil of more than afternoon mist. The end of Auden's verse came back to me: "Scenes we remember as unchanging because there we changed."

In the Taipei airport, thinking of the tree and the friends I had seen once more, I finally understood my experience, in its simplicity, and wrote a few lines on the back of a Burger King place mat:

> *Something had happened once,*
> *but what it was*
> *escaped me like the rack*
> *of morning dreams, or mist*
> *on Yangmingshan.*

> *You walked away, and lost yourselves*
> *in darkening air and traffic. I saw*
> *what it had really been was love.*

On furlough from the Army in 1959, I visited Zermatt, Switzerland, and saw the Matterhorn, from a safe distance.

Above: On maneuvers and looking like soldiers for once are Ted Wetzler, Klaus Lorenzen, M.F. (for Millard Fillmore) Kershner, Charlie Smith, Bill Manly, and Bill Bridges. At left, I sew on my new Spec.4 patch. Below: A convivial evening in Würzburg with our CO, Capt. James Wingate, and Max Nichols.

Above: Karen's parents, Mary and Fritz, on Fritz's 80th birthday. Below and right: Karen before and after Oxydol. She cleaned up well.

'. . . and mean-
while, we have
had a wedding
day . . .'

Dec. 30, 1962

Photos by David W. Jackson

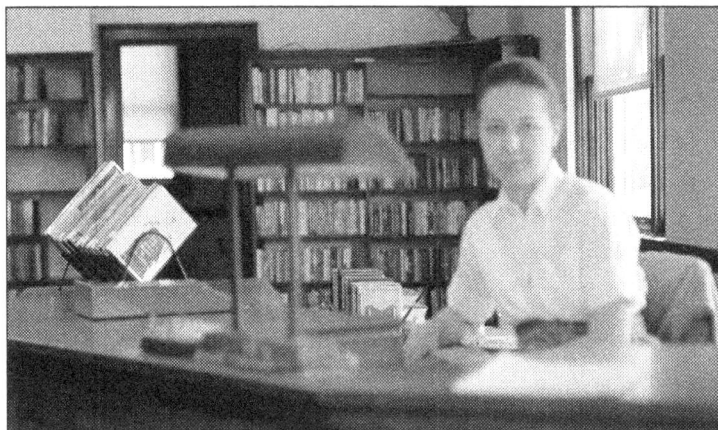

Above: Karen at North Branch Library in Vincennes, 1963. Right: With David and Karl. Below: Newlywed caffeine addicts.

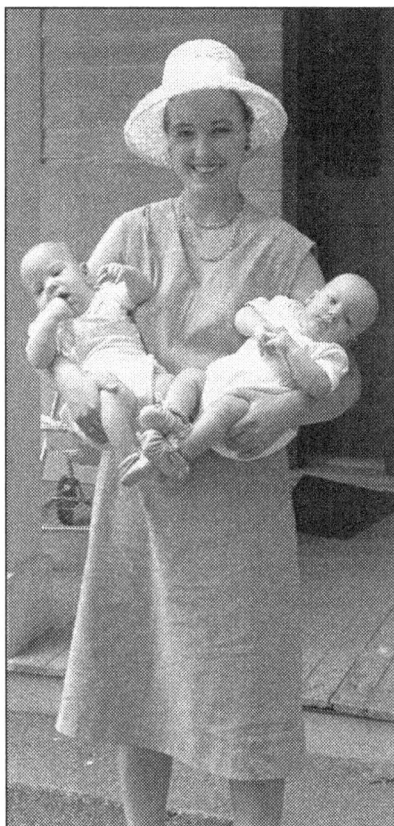

In Venice: Karen, David, and Karl (front) feed pigeons in the Piazzetta near the church of St. Mark, in the background, and the Doge's Palace, right, during a trip to Europe in 1974.

METRO EDITION   Louisville, Ky., Some morning, July, 1979   20¢

The Courier-Journal

Shortage of qualified faculty cited

Franklin College will close by December; Journalism first to go in cutback of 'frills'

The closing at a glance

Well-heeled grand jury finds boots case a shoe-in

The misanthrope and the pterodactyl: a cautionary tale

A mock front page was prepared for Bill's departure from the Louisville *Courier-Journal* in 1979. The staff did a vast amount of work, including the obtaining of an architect's drawing of a proposed building from the college's files. These were top-flight investigative reporters.

Photo by Andrea Betts

Touched by an angel? No, just by the Indiana Collegiate Press Association at Ball State University, which had honored the Franklin College newspaper. From left: Adviser Bill Bridges, Blythe Richards, editor Kim Tibbs, Courtney Swinford, Renee Kean, and Melissa Stewart.

94

Staff of the *Free China Journal*, 1994. in the paper's newsroom in the Government Information Office building, 2 Tientsin St., Taipei. From left: Executive editor Vance Chang, Diana Lin, Sam Dixon (back), Virginia Sheng, Deborah Shen, Allen Pun, managing editor Wendy Lin, Kelly Her, Venny Chan, Bill Bridges, and Jessica Chen.

Archaeological Team No. 5 to St. Kilda in the Outer Hebrides, summer of 2000. Seated from left: Bill Bridges, team leader Fiona Black, Caroline Hirst, Ann Wakeling, Charles Martin. Standing: Falgunee Sarker, archaeologists Marcia Taylor and Bob Will, Joroen van der Stok, Tom Miller (cook), Stuart Hughes, Vicky Marsh, and Donald Reid. We are wearing the cords with our bottle cap "citations."

CHAPTER 15

Art Around the Corner

For 10 weeks in the summer of 1993, en route to Taiwan, I lived in an art gallery—or to put it more accurately, I lived around the corner from one and spent every possible moment there, until I knew every picture by heart and its location. I was able to do this because a young man in my rooming house worked at the gallery and had gotten me a pass by explaining that I was his father.

There may be a corresponding false pretense in anything I say about art, but the subject is important to me—and how many people get to live in an art gallery, other than artists? I am a little like a homeless man who has come in from the cold and who, once his hands have warmed and the frost is off his mustache, has looked around to see what is going on among these bits of colored canvas on the walls. My response is a direct and emotional one—I have only a limited intellectual grasp of the subject.

Oh, no, I can hear a knowledgeable reader saying, another of those tiresome people who don't know anything about art, but "know what they like." But the case is more complicated than this. I don't go into an art gallery knowing what I like and looking for repetitions of it, nor do I go to admire the artist's brushwork or mastery of perspective, which are closed books to me. I go to be surprised, intrigued, moved, or just pleased.

97

My first such moment was a half-century ago at the top of a dark staircase in a cloister outside Florence. Coming up into the light, I found myself face to face—from a distance of four feet—with Fra Angelico's *Annunciation to the Virgin.* I recognized it from an art-history class I'd taken as a schedule-filler in college. And here was the thing itself, hung carelessly, it seemed, in a hallway where the brothers brushed by it on their way to breakfast or prayer. I didn't need a guide! All I had to do was look!

At the Phillips Museum in Washington, D.C., where I had my pass, I could look all I wanted at Renoir's *Luncheon of the Boating Party*, which I did with great pleasure. But what I stared at for a long time was a small Picasso drypoint of horses (*The Watering Place*, 1905), or rather Picasso's *suggestion* of horses—a few spare lines, barely there, that said, "This is what horses are—it is everything you need to know."

At the Eiteljorg Museum in Indianapolis is a painting by the southwestern artist Victor Higgins, who grew up in Shelbyville, Indiana, next door to my home of Franklin. I have no idea how art critics rate Higgins, although the Eiteljorg seems to think well of him. His painting *Palo Duro Canyon* makes me catch my breath every time I see it. He has somehow managed to paint the *space* between the canyon rim and distant trees. I feel in danger of falling.

Not long after my encounter in the hallway with Fra Angelico's angel, I had the good luck to spend a few days in the home of a Yugoslav artist, Vilko Gecan, in Zagreb. (The parents of my Army friend Bill Manly had known the Gecans from a transatlantic crossing in the 1930s, and we were invited to visit.) Vilko was quite old and palsy had shattered his hands, but as the trembling grew worse he had simplified his technique so that a few splashes of color became a table and flowers. He introduced Bill and me to slivovitz—plum brandy— poured from his World War I wooden army canteen, and sent us home with sketches and a painting.

(Bill and I were also introduced to a Gecan family friend, Buba Bertolino, with whom we both fell half in love. We had never met a teen-ager before who was not only beautiful but also fluent in four languages.)

Vilko was regarded as a Yugoslav national treasure, though I haven't run across his work in museums elsewhere. I once asked my artist uncle, Stephen, why some fine artists are world-famous and others aren't. He was kind enough not to laugh at my naiveté—it can be a matter, he said, of luck, of skill in self-promotion, of being in the right place. He did not try to explain degrees of genius. What he and Vilko taught me, again, was just to look, and to consult the guidebook later if at all. (When my family and I visited Venice, where Stephen had been dozens of times, he did not load us with art criticism—he told us where to find the Tiepolos.)

I am not denigrating study and knowledgeability in art. I would be a better viewer if I knew more. But it's unfortunate when people are intimidated by art or think there is nothing there for them. This is the tyranny of the expert. Go look, I want to say; art, like literature, belongs to you, too.

I don't expect them to like the same things I do. Karen is not as taken with Victor Higgins as I am. My son Colin is an excellent artist, and a few years ago we went to see an exhibit of Mughal art from medieval India. (It was the "King of the World" exhibit.) These jeweled fantasies affected me greatly and later got into a poem, but I sensed they were not Colin's big interest at that moment. I had dragged him off to look at *my* enthusiasm. (When I asked him about this recently, he confirmed it. The Mughal art was fine, but what had struck *him* were the Alexander Calder mobiles.)

I am surprised how often the visual arts have found their way into poems of mine. There is an affinity here of some kind, though not always well expressed. As a writer, I sometimes try to read a narrative into a picture, when I should just gaze at it. (My poem "Narrative" touches on this problem.) From the summer in the Phillips I have a bad short story inspired by Richard Diebenkorn's *Girl With Plant* (1960). The painting is quite enough without my elaboration. When I am simply registering the emotional shock of an artwork, the results are better.

And surely there is no reason to be embarrassed by an emotional response, although some experts are. For a newspaper feature, I once interviewed a curator at the Indianapolis Museum of Art about the work of William Merritt Chase.

Chase was born near Franklin, but left as soon as he could for Europe and later the East Coast; the museum was featuring an exhibit of his work.

I had boned up and the curator answered my questions patiently. It was late on a Friday—the interview was going nowhere. In desperation, I said, "But don't some critics fault Chase for lacking inventiveness and regarding art as just 'a fine manufacture'?" Yes, the curator said, some feel that Chase fails to stir the viewer. "But I love his work because it is *beautiful*, not because it involves me emotionally." She went on, with emotion, to defend Chase, and the interview was saved.

My interest in art does not extend very far into music. I seem to have a mainly visual imagination and am not good at mathematics. I enjoy recitals and concerts (trying to take my own advice not to be intimidated), but what I remember are the non-musical details, like the little girl in Berlin, waiting raptly in her concert-hall box for her father to strike his one note on the triangle. Or, in Taipei, getting a ride to the bus stop with Mstislav Rostropovich's chauffeur, on his way to pick up the maestro after a performance. I warmed his seat for him! Or the cellist called back so many times that he finally peeked around the curtain as if to say, "Haven't you people gone home yet?"

Karen and I attended a Vivaldi concert in the composer's home church in Venice, but my interest was nearly as much in the thunderstorm crashing in time with the music and in the lightning playing among the high windows. Long ago in Germany, I tried to educate myself with the help of a musician friend, who recommended starting with pieces by the pianist Wilhelm Backhaus. I got a Backhaus record and listened, but my interest soon waned. I have a good record collection—inherited—with the classics and some special giants like Henry Purcell. But I seldom listen to them and should donate the records to someone who would. My fault, my most grievous fault.

I've just dug out and looked again at the notebook I kept to help locate the pictures (about 120 of them) in the Phillips during that summer of 1993. Some of the names mean little now, but others are still vivid. I made brief notes on some and an extensive one on *Marseilles, Gateway to the Orient* (1868)

by Pierre Puvis de Chavannes: "An endlessly mysterious painting. People on a boat (but who are those shadowy, giant figures?). The old Orthodox priest reading his Bible. The woman
in yellow standing calmly against the rail. The man like a
gladiator in the foreground. What this stirs is a recollection of
childhood, of using an old footstool, turned over, as a boat.
This ship with its heavy rail is like that."

I did not neglect the Phillips's modern collection and cop-
ied down a comment by the artist Myron Stout posted next to a
charcoal drawing: "Atomic painting is what I do. Every bloody
atom has to be painted individually! I may think I'm working
in a macrocosmic vein, but that's a mistake. It's microcosmic
and a plague on it!"

What a note of asperity, suggesting the Talmudic description of the task that can be neither completed nor abandoned.

In a gallery in Florence (the Accademia, I think) is a painting of a burning city. In the foreground a dwarf looks out at the
viewer and gestures with a lantern toward the scene. I don't
know the artist or the name of the painting, although I could
probably find them. But the dwarf has made his way into a
poem that is one way of looking at what an artist does:

> He was inventing the world. Each day
> resolved itself in his gaze
> as a painting starts
> from the eye of the helmeted
> man in the foreground, his hand raised
> toward a prospect of smoke and horses,
> his mouth beginning to form
> a word: "Behold!"

I live in a house full of art I love, much of it made by people I know and love. There are paintings and stained glass by
my Uncle Stephen, and a one-time venture in glass—a basket-
ball player—by my father. There is a photograph of Deacon
Brodie's pub in Edinburgh by a teaching colleague, Susie
Fleck, as well as two nautical scenes by a Scottish friend,
Edwin Wakeling. Two etchings by Charles A. Vanderhoof
were a gift from the artist's daughters to my Uncle Bill. I'm

especially pleased by several paintings and linoleum-block prints from Colin. One is called *Spaceship #1* and shows a craft that appears tethered to earth by gluey footpads. But lights shine through it, and I have decided it is a stargate, to the future perhaps.

Another of Colin's prints is an abstract, and Karen and I were perplexed about which way to hang it. I finally noticed what appeared to be a smiley face—surely the artist's directional clue. "Why did you hang it upside down," Colin said the next time he came through. And then, "Never mind—this is the way you saw it." He hadn't noticed the smiley face.

I go into every gallery I can and treat everything with respect and nothing with awe. A few months ago, I went to Chicago for a business lunch in the café of the Art Institute. I got to the institute a couple of hours early and went looking. I found a painter I didn't know, Paul Delvaux, and gazed at his haunted portrayals of women. There was a roomful of Joseph Cornell "boxes"—little cabinets with constructions of found objects. I had liked Cornell for a long time, but this display deepened my understanding of the variety in his art.

There is no end to this. After living at the Phillips for nine weeks and making my own road map to each of its rooms, I came in one Monday and found that the whole museum had been rearranged over the weekend. Almost everything I knew had been carted off to storage, and a whole new array had appeared. I was outraged for a moment, then amused, and finally intrigued. What were all these interesting new colored scraps that someone had hung on the walls of my room?

"Gail Beverly," by Vilko Gecan, Chicago, 1927

Bill and Buba Bertolino

Anka and Vilko Gecan

INTERVAL: YUKON DAYS

Newspaper readers bring in the damnedest things.

One brought in newspapers from Gold Rush days in the Klondike, where a relative had been a prizefighter. Years later, I used some academic prize money to visit the Yukon Archives in Whitehorse and examine the *Yukon Morning Journal*, which lasted only three months in 1901, but made the most of it.

Of a civic campaign for moral uplift, it wrote: "Since time was a callow youth, attired only in the scanty garb of inexperience, there have been drunkards and there have been gamblers. When the scythe of time, grown old and decrepit, shall have rusted and fallen from its haft, and Gabriel blows his last horn, there will be those who will be drunk and cannot respond, and those who will stop to see the next card."

The *Journal* delighted in whimsy, delivered without too much regard for fact. Some Yukon papers responded to dull news days by reporting the discovery of Noah's Ark on nearby mountains. The *Journal* recounted the finding of a watch chain under 45 feet of gravel—"evidence of prehistoric man." It chronicled a "pasty war" between bill plasterers for rival theaters. "The word lobster has been spoken," it noted ominously.

The *Journal* also told of a prospector who assured himself of both supple shoe leather and bread by leaving sourdough to rise overnight in his boots. Another miner, the paper reported to its readers, walked for three days "against the whirl of the earth" and found himself 4,000 miles from home.

One day another reader walked into my office carrying a battered fiddle with a label inside saying (in Latin) "Antonio Stradivarius made me" and a date. I carried it around for weeks in the trunk of my car before getting to an expert who reassured me it was a fake. The last two digits of the date were printed; Stradivarius left those digits blank, to be filled in at the time of manufacture. "Of course," the expert added, "serious crooks know this and have labels with blank digits."

Newspaper readers are wonderful. They even bring in potatoes shaped like Calvin Coolidge.

CHAPTER 16

A Contact Sport

"The rain pings on my helmet, and then it goes through all the holes and my brain goes soggy." This is Ann Wakeling of Aviemore, Scotland, responding to my request for a description of the weather as she bicycled from Land's End to John o' Groats. Ann is a letter writer with a "voice"—informative and funny, with her own wry slant on things. Her letter *was* the writer, present in the room as I read—and you will hear more about her in a later chapter.

Another correspondent, in an e-mail, described "friends trapped in miserable relationships which are going nowhere. They do a wonderful job rationalizing men's inattention or rudeness. You will be shocked to know that education and brilliance in a woman do not always translate into savvyness in the realm of dating."

I'm shocked, and cannot resist quoting her a little further, about her own concept of the Fabulous Girl, or FG:

"An FG is someone who is liberated but chic, impeccably mannered but never a snob, confident but compassionate, full of verve instead of vanity—you get the picture."

I certainly do. Not all correspondents write with this much grace and wit, nor do they have to. The quiet friend is as valued as the one who sets off fireworks, in some moods more so. The medium doesn't matter: two lines of e-mail may be just what I need today. I treasure a letter scrawled on a purple napkin in a bowling alley by a new daughter-in-law. While my son was competing in his league, she was rolling a 300 game with his father. The best message is always "I'm thinking of you." Greeting-card makers figured it out long ago.

Timing is important. My Uncle Bill, possibly the best correspondent I've known, once wrote that "replying by return mail is the sign of an idle mind." He was replying by return mail at the time. But letting too much time go by can be fatal. There are people I'd love to hear from again, but I've let the fire go out under the epistolary boiler, and it's too late to relight it. In an essay on this subject a few years ago, an author told of a distinguished friend whose letter he had let go unanswered. After a month or so, he said, answering properly would have required half a day of artful apologies and witty narrative. After another six months it would have required a visit to the British Museum. He never answered and the friend died.

Between some writers, a comfortable interval develops. With an editor friend, letters go back and forth every month or so. With an Army buddy, now a Chaucer scholar, it's two to three months (although the pace has picked up lately). With my step-sister in Hawaii (Hi, Sally!), it's half a year. Much longer than that, though, and we're talking Christmas cards.

This may sound as if I have correspondents by the dozen, but I don't. The number of regulars is rather small. As one celebrity put it: "No one can maintain a meaningful relationship with 9,000 fans in Finland." And the reasons for corresponding vary. Sometimes I just want to hear a friendly voice, or be one myself. With a few writers, I share intense interests that demand frequent pages of information, opinions, speculation, suggestions, hand-wringing, and hand-holding. In very rare instances, the correspondent fills both roles, of friend and colleague, and then the fortunate recipient has what the Chinese call a *chih-yin*: the friend, the reader, who understands my heart.

This is not intended to be a letter-writing manual, as if anyone could learn the art from a manual. It's just a few observations you can take or leave.

I've heard people bemoan e-mail as the death of letter writing, but I love the idea that I can sit down and send words instantly to someone on the far side of the world. I'm a words-on-the-page person, not a phone person. E-mails can be as thoughtfully written as any letter, or can be dashed off with the haste of a Post-It note, misspellings and all. I love my Taiwan correspondent who kindly labors in hesitant English, because my Chinese is so much worse. "Everything's OK," she writes. "I'm fun." Well, of course she is—and if you're reading this, dear France, please don't ever change that wonderful "fun" to "fine."

I also love everything about regular or "snail mail." It's a ritual, from selecting the paper to typing the letter (sometimes over several days or weeks) to visiting the post office and buying the right stamp, then picturing the letter as it wings its way over mountain, plain, and sea. Such letters can be written on the computer, but now and then I turn to Uncle Bill's 1923 Remington #16, with his note still on the front, reminding him (and now me) that the brackets are the reverse of what the key-tops say. Fix them? Never. I was touring a steamboat, now a museum, in the Yukon, and the guide pointed out the purser's ancient Remington #16. "You don't see those anymore," he said. "Oh, I don't know," I piped up. "I have one next to my computer—use it all the time." The guide's look said, "Geez, you get all kinds on this job."

In letter-writing advice, the old clichés are the best. (Yes, I know, it's time for some sparkling new clichés.) Be yourself, write in your own voice, never be intimidated, never apologize for not writing, have some fun. Some people become someone else when they sit down to write: self-conscious, stuffy, worried about effect. "My God, I'm <u>Writing a Letter!</u>" But even this is contact, so don't be critical of your correspondents. A note to mine: I'm the most uncritical recipient you ever saw. I hunger for mail. I stand on the front porch, tapping my foot, trying to will the postman down the block faster. When your letter is among the bills and other junk mail, I am the happiest of men.

Managing even a small correspondence takes time, but it can be sandwiched in around other things, and there are ways to streamline. (I'm about to give away secrets here.) I keep a list by date of outgoing letters and major e-mails, and who has written but not been answered yet. It's haphazard, but it helps keep me from forgetting friends. And it's fun to look back to see what the traffic was in, say, 1998. Victorian epistolarians kept "letter books," into which went letters received, as well as transcribed copies of outgoing ones. When did they find the time? I use three-ring binders, with plastic sheet protectors, a binder per correspondent. (One writer is now working on Binder No. 10.) Copies are easy; the computer spits them out. If you handwrite a letter, Xerox it for filing. And if you, too, own a Remington #16—well, it will be good to know that I'm not the last person in the civilized world who uses carbon paper. (You can, of course, keep computer files of letters, but I like to pull down a binder and savor the whole body of the exchange. And the binders never crash.)

Saving e-mails on the computer is easy, but I print them out and slip them into the sheet protectors. It takes a minute or two, but it works. Sometimes the old technology is best. My executor can throw them all out, but meanwhile I can look back and enjoy. And it keeps me from repeating myself more than I already do.

Handwritten letters: They're great, personal, and I love to get them, even when it takes my Captain Midnight Magic Decoder Ring to puzzle out the handwriting. But it's content that counts, and there's nothing impersonal to me about a typed letter. Uncle Bill wrote them all the time, endearingly.

A favorite correspondent, plagued by carpal tunnel syndrome, tried turning her writing over to a voice-activated device, called Viva Voce, I believe. This produced some crazily misspelled and dyslexic missives that often had a nutty logic of their own. Happily, my correspondent's hands are working again, but I pine occasionally for Miss Viva's wonderful weirdness.

Don't overwhelm your readers. Most letters longer than three pages have overstayed their welcome, although there are many exceptions. Look back at your friend's last letter or e-mail and answer any questions. This also confirms that you actually read it. Express a little interest in what the friend is doing. Don't whine, complain about your sad life, or overdo the medical details. I do want to know the troubles and worries of my friends, and to tell them my own. But it's best, except *in extremis*, to strike a note of Bravely Carrying On.

Almost anything can go into a letter—deep seriousness, fun, compassion, High Silliness— as long as it's in the writer's true voice. In fact, more than that can go in. For a while one correspondent was dropping a handful of glitter stars into her envelopes. When my wife and I spotted an envelope from her, a cry went up: "It's a letter from Susanna! Get a newspaper!"

As in any relationship, there are times for silence, to give the other party a chance to reflect or to do something besides write, like eating or the laundry. E-mail exchanges are especially vulnerable to wild escalation until both participants collapse, panting. One of my correspondents, the poet Mike O'Connor, has translated these lines from the T'ang Dynasty poet Chia Tao:

> *Separated by water,*
> *we'll be in each other's thoughts—*
> *but no letters to disturb*
> *a monk's quiet life.*

The best book ever written based on letters may be Helene Hanff's *84 Charing Cross Road*, which was made into a movie starring Anne Bancroft. A close second is *The Delicacy and Strength of Lace*, letters between the writers Leslie Marmon Silko and James Wright. These are just my own choices, of course.

And now I've reached or exceeded my three-page limit. But I want to say something more. It's sad to lose correspondents by neglect, but still sadder when it's to the permanency of death. I miss Helen Patrick, who wrote to me about unicorns and passed on delectable 50-year-old gossip from Vincennes, Indiana, my hometown. And Hazel King, a retired librarian from Victoria, B.C., who traveled the world on tramp steamers. And I miss Bob Irick in Taipei. I once wrote Bob that my wife and I were "pecking away" at adjacent keyboards. He replied, "I thought you two were beyond such romantic nonsense." There is a deep poignancy to such extinguished voices, no matter how hopeful we may be that they are still speaking somewhere. "The authors are in eternity," wrote William Blake, although he perhaps had another meaning in mind.

Most of all, I miss my uncle's letters. Bill and I began corresponding when I was still "young Bill," in midlife and busy. He was retired and living quietly in a house in a wood. But his mind ranged freely, over the experiences of a lifetime and over books, nature, and especially the joys and curiosities of language. I've just looked again at my last letter from him, a shorty dated March 15, 1984. He had heard something about one of my students winning a national competition "for a sentence that seemed to make sense but didn't."

"But who? What? When? Where?" he wrote. "If you know, can you send me a Xerox?"

The student was Rachel Sheeley, the fine writer mentioned in an earlier chapter, who had taken first prize in a "bad writing" contest. It was too late to get a copy to Bill, but I can hardly wait to tell him.

CHAPTER 17

The Other Woman

Over the years, Karen has noticed the disparity in numbers between my male and female correspondents: male, a few; female, more than a few. (God, this woman is quick!)

I have carefully explained that these are correspondents, not co-respondents, and she has been good about not using terms like "postal patooties" or "e-mail harem." But I feel the time has finally arrived to come clean, and so I am addressing the following to the one out there who is *prima inter pares.* You know who you are.

Dear _____ :

How are you? I am fine. Karen sends her love.

We have been writing these letters to each other for years now, not to mention e-mails, and I wanted you to know that I have enjoyed them very much, and value your friendship and attention, even though we almost never meet. Thank you.

It has occurred to me that, with all the postal fun, there has never been an unambiguous declaration from me of my feelings for you. So here it is at long last:

☞ DECLARATION ☜

If I were to choose one person with whom to have an absolutely hopeless Grand Passion, a towering and mythic ro-

111

mance, destroying lives and scattering psychic wreckage for miles in all directions, a legendary *Liebesturm*, replete with dramatic tableaux—the hand thrown across the brow in despair, the wild tears at midnight, the message saying, "Flee, all is discovered!" . . .

Or if, eschewing theatrics, I were to choose someone for whom to take the vow of silent and noble renunciation, being always present in the background to perform small acts of service, but never breathing my unrequited passion, except to one faithful (and highly gifted) friend, who would write an immortal ode about it, long after both our deaths. . . .

Or if, instead, we *both* were to take the path of high epic story, abandoning everything—honor, the world, our immortal souls—for the pure oriflamme of a sin so huge, so wickedly delicious, so Heloise-Abelard, that in the end we would have to retire to separate monasteries and spend our few remaining days in ceaseless acts of prayer and contrition. . . .

If, as I say, I were to choose one person with whom to do any or all of the above (and assuming this person was idiot enough to agree) . . . my dear, it would be you.

But since our respective spouses would both have to approve, I suppose there's not much chance of this happening.

Faithfully yours,

Bill

CHAPTER 18

The Road to Everywhere

I have just two words for you—Machu Picchu." Karen and I were having Easter morning coffee in 1995 with the college chaplain, Cliff Cain, after his sunrise service. Who spoke the two words—Cliff or me—has never been quite clear. But both of us had always wanted to visit the Inca city in the Andes. And when academics want to go somewhere, the next two words are likely to be "student trip."

Cliff was a whiz at arranging such trips, and I knew how to publicize them. On Jan. 18, 1997, the two of us with 16 others were standing amid the clouds, mists, and mountains of Machu Picchu—just 21 months and two days after our Easter breakfast.

I didn't start out to be a world traveler. I admired Thoreau's remark, "I have traveled widely in Concord." But for 10 years after my first visit to Taipei in 1992, I seemed to be in perpetual transit. To a year in Taipei (1993-4) and a return visit in 1996 were added Japan, Peru, Canada, Germany (twice, with a side trip to Poland), Australia, Scotland, Cornwall, and the remote Scottish island of St. Kilda. A final trip went even further, at least symbolically, to the Kennedy Space Center in Florida, where NASA had invited students to watch the launch of *Columbia*'s repair mission to the Hubble telescope. (A few months later, the same spacecraft disintegrated on re-entry, killing its crew.) When not traveling abroad, I was going off to meetings in this country—Canadian studies and journalism conferences, seminars on computer-assisted reporting, poetry festivals.

The trip to Machu Picchu in Peru included, besides Cliff and me, a third professor, 13 students, and Cliff's 12-year-old daughter. Also my sister-in-law Nancy, a professional photographer and a diminutive dervish of energy and determination. We flew into Cuzco in the Andes and then went by a little yellow train down the Urubamba river valley to Machu Picchu, where we stayed at a tourist hotel just outside the Inca ruins.

The poet William Bronk, making a similar trip, remarked that all other attributes of the Andes have been suppressed in favor of verticality, of rising. And it is true; as night fell over the ruins, the mountains seemed to crowd closer and loom above us. The site was almost deserted, and occasional streamers of mist rose from the valley 2,000 feet below. The day-trippers had gone, and Cliff and I walked alone through an empty city of exquisitely cut stone, once gray but now softened by lichens to browns and faint greens. This was what we had come for.

The next morning, some of us climbed Huayna Picchu, the sugarloaf mountain that appears in the background of most photographs of Machu Picchu. On the way down, my group lost its way briefly, and we found ourselves scrambling over ruined Inca terraces seven feet high. "Shit!" I heard the demure divinity student behind me gasping. "Shit! I'll never make it!"

Later that day, we reboarded the train for Cuzco, but partway there it stopped. My sister-in-law Nancy, never one to sit idly, went forward to see what was wrong. She came back to report that an oil gasket had blown, but that the engine crew had used her Swiss Army Knife to whittle a new one. The train began to move again. Soon after that, Nancy became violently ill and threw up her socks all the way to Cuzco, where Cliff and I virtually carried her off the train. A doctor was summoned at midnight to administer shots for food poisoning and maybe a little *soroche*, or altitude sickness. About 3 a.m. the doctor returned. Some students had gone night-clubbing, forgetting that Cuzco is several thousand feet higher than Machu

Picchu. More *soroche* shots were given to members of what became known as the Sore Butt Club.

The next morning, Nancy appeared, wan and wobbly, but still game for a noon interview with a museum director. The interview perked her up a bit, as did a little chicken soup. A photo exhibit brought more improvement, and an afternoon of shopping completed the cure. At 11 p.m., I was collapsing, but Nancy was still looking for more coffee beans to buy.

From Cuzco we flew to Lima for an unexpected high point of the trip, the "Lord of Sipan" exhibit at the National Museum—Peruvian treasures just back from a tour of Europe and New York. During the trip, I had compiled a little exhibit of my own. My son Colin had loaned me his heavy windbreaker, and the students and I photographed it all over the Andes— draped over Inca walls, at the Temple of the Virgins of the Sun, and at a Cuzco restaurant where the students toasted the coat with pisco sours. I put the pictures together with a narrative, titled it *Colin's Coat Visits Peru,* and gave it to him.

During the trip we had most of the problems that can befall student groups. One student disclosed she was pregnant, which didn't stop her from jumping off Inca walls. Another had a kidney infection, and another fell in love with a Peruvian soldier and had to be kept on the tour almost by force. But we had eaten wonderful Andean food and drunk several gallons of Inca Cola. And we had seen Machu Picchu!

In fact, it had been so much fun that Karen and I took Cliff out for coffee the next Easter, and I repeated our mantra: "I have just two words (or possibly three) for you—Australia 2000!" This time I handled travel arrangements, which became dicey as the date neared. Australia would be the college's farthest and most expensive January "winter term" trip. I had managed to bring the cost in at under $3,000 for each student. But then a demand for flights, apparently from jet-setters bent on being airborne during the Y2K crisis, caused airlines to raise prices. The students were so set on Australia that they kicked in more money, as did the college. During a brief moment when costs and income were in balance, I signed the contract and we were on our way.

115

FIVE-MOUNTAIN MORNING

The Australia trip included several non-students, Karen among them this time. We explored Sidney, visited the Blue Mountains for a taste of the outback, and toured the tablelands above the city of Cairns in Queensland. We spent a day on the Great Barrier Reef, where students thought it sweet that Karen and I snorkeled hand in hand. They didn't know that her first mask had leaked and that she was holding on for fear of drowning. There was only one emergency this time. A student left his wallet, passport, and every scrap of ID in a restaurant; luckily, it was still there when he went back.

Between Peru and Australia, another professor and I had taken students to Canada—again during the January winter term. Our travel agent, not used to groups touring in mid-winter, still managed to find sights and programs for us in Quebec, Montreal, Ottawa, and Toronto. We reached Canada a week after the great ice storm of 1998. Workmen were still chipping ice off Montreal's Notre Dame cathedral and our train crept past miles of shattered trees and fallen power lines. But we had a good time and saw a hockey game in Ottawa. This time the only emergency occurred when a student tried to enter the Canadian Parliament with a semicircular butterfly knife in his pocket. He had forgotten all about it; security police grilled him for a while before returning him to us, unharmed and un-armed.

Sandwiched among these trips, Karen and I also did some traveling for pleasure and literary reasons. In 1992, on the way back from my VIP trip to Taipei, we met in Japan and visited Tokyo, Kyoto, and the western cities of Matsue and Kanazawa. I wrote several poems about Kyoto; Matsue was of interest as the last home of an Irish-Greek-American journalist, Lafcadio Hearn, who had done much to introduce Japan to western readers.

In August, 1997, we took another literary-pleasure trip, this time starting in Scotland. We saw the annual tattoo, or military review, at Edinburgh Castle, then took a train to Aberdeen (a severe city of stone and roses) and to Inverness, which we fell in love with permanently. A bus took us along Loch Ness to the monastery where my Uncle Stephen had been a novice for a time in the 1930s.

THE ROAD TO EVERYWHERE

From Inverness, a train whisked us in a day to Cornwall, at the other end of Great Britain, where a favorite poet, W.S. Graham, had spent much of his writing life. I wanted to chase down some obscure place names in his poems. A bookstore clerk in Penzance knew them all, had actually known Graham, and put me in touch with his literary executors, Margaret and Michael Snow, who have been correspondents ever since.

Back at the college, a call came early in 1999, asking if Franklin could provide five journalism students for a study tour of Germany, concentrating on Berlin and Hamburg. And if so, would I like to be the U.S. leader of 25 students from five American schools? I agreed, and Karen again went along at her own expense. In Berlin, the students and I did a rigorous round of interviews with journalists and politicians; a German friend took Karen on an equally rigorous walking tour of Berlin. Together we revisited some spots I remembered from UPI almost 40 years before. Joe Fleming's old office was gone, but the Kurfürstendamm in spring was as lovely a street as ever, and the quality of German beer had not deteriorated. (Two years later I made the same study trip again, visiting Berlin, Hamburg, and Frankfurt/Oder, with an excursion across the river into Poland.)

The trip to the 2002 space-shuttle launch came about because another professor had applied to a NASA student-press program. We didn't expect to be chosen, and the invitation (for two teachers and two students) came only days before the launch. We rushed about, getting approvals, covering our classes, and loading up with cameras and electronic gear. NASA bused us to a close-in press site for the pre-dawn launch. A photographer had showed me just which buttons to push, and I got some spectacular photos that we sent back on the internet, with stories, for the next day's student newspaper.

I liked one liftoff photo so much that I signed and framed it. My sister-in-law Nancy saw it later on a wall and cocked her photographer's eye. "That's a beautiful picture, Bill," she said, "but you really shouldn't sign something you didn't take." "But I did take it!" I cried. Nancy, for once, was speechless.

Sometime in this period, it became clear that I had acquired a reputation as a traveler. "So where are you going

next?" people would ask. One day (I think it was after Australia), the publisher of our local newspaper said, "I'm going to
put an item in the personals column: 'Professor Bridges paid
one of his rare visits to Franklin this week.'"

Was I was overdoing it? A friend had said of another well-
traveled colleague, "What is this man running from?" And yet,
except for the year's leave in Taipei, the travel hadn't taken me
away for any substantial time from classes or other college
work—in fact some of it had been connected with classwork. I
dismissed the publisher's gibe, and began planning the most
unusual journey yet, to "the island at the edge of the world."

**Cliff Cain, co-leader on the Peruvian
trip, holds up Colin's coat at Machu
Picchu. Our group later climbed Huayna Picchu, the peak in the background.**

CHAPTER 19

The Edge of the World

After a bumpy night on the North Atlantic, I stumbled up from a "coffin bunk" on the 70-foot motorship *Poplar Diver* and saw the steep, stony, and treeless hills of St. Kilda all around me. It was the summer of 2000 and the end of a journey that had begun more than 10 years earlier in the pages of a 1911 encyclopedia.

Then, I had been researching a place even more remote: the barren Atlantic seamount of Rockall. St. Kilda caught my eye because, unlike Rockall, people *had* lived there—77 of them in 1901, by the encyclopedia's count. Cut off by wintry seas for eight months of the year, the islanders lived on birds: gannets, fulmars, puffins. The world's last great auk had been killed there in 1840 by two bird hunters who thought it was a witch. The St. Kildans sent "sea messages" in floating boxes, which might eventually wash up on the shore of Scotland's Outer Hebrides 40 miles to the east and be read by someone. It sounded like an interesting place. I wrote a poem about Rockall's utter isolation, and mentioned in passing the sturdy St. Kildans.

Why this fascination with remote islands? It may have started on the same trip to Venice that jolted me into poetry. Beyond Venice, distant in the lagoon, were what W.D. Howells had called "the evanescent islands," and another writer "the islets, small as boats." Baron Corvo, mad for anything Venetian, had tallied these faraway specks: La Grazie, Sanctemente, Santospirito, Sanzorzi in Alga, and also "the various pirogues of the finance." I added my own description: "A scythe of islands garnering a sea." I also wrote a poem around this time, titled "Land's End," which was set in the Pacific, not Venice. It read in part:

> *One thinks of ends,*
> *last rocks and selvages, the skerry*
> *beyond the last island in a chain,*
> *French Frigate Shoal,*
> *skirl in the water,*
>
> *the continents pared down*
> *to a foothold,*
> *last purchase of earth,*
> *telling us what earth is.*

I didn't think much more about St. Kilda, but a desire for "edge places" was growing in me. As a VIP visitor to Taiwan in 1992, I stayed an extra week to visit Hualien, a seacoast city. There, in a room nearly as bare as a monk's cell, I lay at night, listening to rain drip from an eave. I had never been farther away from home, in miles or psychically.

Other journeys, I see now, were leading to St. Kilda. Karen and I went to Matsue, on the Sea of Japan, and sailed past Yomegashima, "Island of the Young Wife," no more than a few trees floating on the waves. The poet Basho had written of "islands beyond islands, on the backs of islands." Machu Picchu was not an island, but it fit the pattern—a place far away and difficult to get to. Karen and I had gone to Land's End at the southern extremity of Britain. Not content with that, we took a boat farther out to the Isles of Scilly and looked farther still, past the Bishop's Rock Light and into the empty, un-islanded Atlantic.

In Scotland, I had found a book, *St. Kilda: Island on the Edge of the World*, by Charles Maclean, which brought St. Kilda's story up to date. The last 35 residents had been evacuated in 1930. The main St. Kilda islets—Hirte, Dun, Soay, and Boreray—were now a nature and bird preserve owned by the National Trust of Scotland. One could get there by being assigned to a small radar tracking station; by taking one of the occasional and expensive St. Kilda cruises, limited to a daytime stop; or by joining an NTS archaeological work party for a modest fee. The age limit for parties was 70; at 65, I still had time. Joining the society to underscore my interest, I applied, was accepted, and told to be on the dock in the western Scottish city of Oban by 4 p.m. on July 7, 2000. Everything after that would depend on weather, the letter said.

Friends wondered what had gotten into me. Sally Hanley, a professor who knew Scotland well, applauded but said, "You do realize, don't you, that St. Kilda is cold and bleak with incessant rain and wind—and that's in high summer." The doctor who okayed me for the trip said, "Did you volunteer for this, or were you sentenced?"

The two weeks on Hirte turned out to be memorable and not at all bleak; even the weather was pleasant. The island did not seem terribly remote or difficult; thanks to the NTS and the radar station, we ate well and had hot showers. One could even get a drink at the Puff Inn, a room next to the radar billets. What made it memorable for me were the 12 other people in Work Party No. 5, of whom 11 were from Great Britain and one from the Netherlands. Fiona Black was our official NTS leader. Bob Will and Marcia Taylor were professional archaeologists, and Tom Miller was our kilted cook. The other nine of us ranged from seasoned amateur diggers to several like me with no experience at all. I've been in many work situations, from smooth to wildly dysfunctional; this was the only one where there was no apparent friction at all, but rather an instant liking for each other. In two weeks, I didn't hear a backbiting remark.

Part of it, I suppose, was that we all felt amazed and blessed to be in this starkly beautiful place, no more than two miles in any direction, with its central mountain and cliffs that dropped 1,000 feet to the sea. And perhaps part was that archaeology makes you too tired to argue. Any romantic ideas I had of unearthing ancient temples vanished during the first day of kneeling on sharp rocks and sorting patiently through hundreds of shards that might have been rough tools, but 99 percent of the time weren't. We amateurs kept running to Bob or

Marcia with finds we thought showed human shaping. "Och," Bob would say in his soft Scottish burr. "I'm so sorrry. It's oonly a stoon." But when a stone did qualify as a tool (and I found the first one—see inset), it had to be minutely described and located in time and space. Every item on a modern archaeological site is computer-mapped.

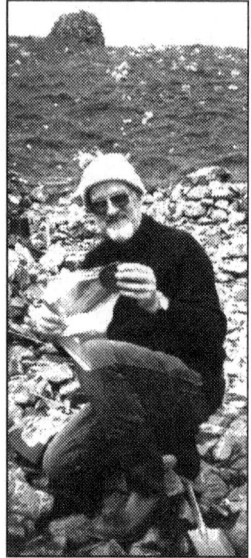

The site itself, which once had been a small gathering of stone huts on a hillside, also had to be painstakingly surveyed. Charlie Martin, a Bristol headmaster, and I teamed up on the theodolite to map inch-by-inch gradations of the ground. One morning he said, "It's strange to think that I know these 10 square meters better than any spot on earth." (Charlie was also an ornithologist and took me along on nighttime bird hikes.) The true treasures of our digging were bits of pottery, often barely distinguishable from the surrounding clay; these had to be lifted out and bagged with care. As we dug into the foundations of the archaic huts, every rock also had to be sketched *in situ* as well as photographed. I asked Marcia why photos weren't enough. Because photos can lie, she explained, with shadows and the angle of view disguising features in the rock wall that are clear to a draftsman. I realized that archaeology is a science of infinite pains. Once disturbed, a site is never exactly the same again. The archaeologist has just one shot at getting it right.

At the end of our two weeks, all the rocks and dirt that had accumulated in heaps around the site had to be put back as nearly as possible in their original places, by a "bucket brigade." An enduring (and endearing) memory is of Vicky Marsh, the slightest of our party, slinging rocks and buckets of dirt and keeping up with everyone else. The result of all this labor: Work Party No. 5 found bits of Early Iron Age pottery from 300 B.C., documenting human settlement on St. Kilda 1,000 years earlier than had been known for sure. Tom Miller, who had cooked for several work parties, said, "This is the hardest-working, happiest, just absolutely bloody luckiest bunch of dirt monkeys I've ever seen." Returning from the dig one day, several of us met some children from a visiting boat. "Are you the archaeologists?" they asked. We looked at each other. "Yes, we are," I said, and then shooed them up the path before they could ask any tough questions.

We were happy for non-archaeological reasons, too. On days off from work, Fiona Black led us on hikes around the island, along trails made by the island's Soay sheep, whose ancestors were the progenitors of all modern breeds. We poked our noses into a few of the hundreds of cleits, small conical stone sheds built by the islanders for storage. We also learned about "bonxies," giant skuas that sometimes dive-bomb hikers. (Caroline Hirst, a young return visitor to St. Kilda, led me in a "bonxie dance" on the beach. As we ran in circles, "airplaning" with our arms, I had seldom felt more foolish or happier.)

Other memories remain: drinking scotch late at night in the stone dining hut (a restored village house, like the ones we slept in); hearing Donald Reid tell of his job as a railway supervisor; and listening to Stuart Hughes, a young BBC reporter, make tapes for later broadcast. I talked about weaving with Ann Wakeling, who became a permanent friend; she gathered wool shed by the Soay sheep, to be cleaned and later spun. Falgunee Sarker and I teamed on hikes; her short legs and my age sometimes made us fall behind the rest, but we looked out for each other. And finally there was our happy Dutchman, Joroen van der Stok, who frightened me by running to the top of a "lover's leap" hundreds of feet above the ocean. Several months later he and Vicky Marsh became engaged—but then Joroen died of a sudden illness, less than a year after leaving St. Kilda.

On our last morning, we posed for a photo and received our "St. Kilda medals"—pop bottle caps strung on twine. I treasure mine like the Croix de Guerre.

The *Poplar Diver* deposited us back in Oban on a Sunday morning after a voyage so calm we could sleep on deck. I could forgo the coffin bunk, an enclosed bed entered feet first through a small opening. While waiting for a bus to join Karen in Inverness, I strolled up Oban's main street. I was dirty, bearded, and wearing a once-gray stocking cap. A man passed me and under his breath said, "Had a hard night, huh, buddy?"

Karen and I did one more quick island hop, to the Orkneys and the ancient settlement of Skara Brae, then went to Edinburgh where I researched St. Kildan poetry in the National Library. It had been an island of singers; an old photo shows one of them, Euphemia MacCrimmon, looking at 84 like a wild North Atlantic Druid priestess. Some of the island's poems are forgettable, and many tell of friends and kin who fell over cliffs. But there is a superb love song that begins:

> *Away bent spade, away straight spade,*
> *away each goat and sheep and lamb;*
> *up my rope, up my snare—*
> *I have heard the gannet upon the sea!*

In my last years at the college, I continued to travel with students. But St. Kilda in some way had assuaged my hunger for the remote and inaccessible. Perhaps it was because I had gone to the edge and found friends there, not loneliness and isolation. Or perhaps I had finally just out-traveled the urge. I had also begun realizing that no place on our shrinking world is very remote, or safe from our actions. St. Kilda is in the news as I write. Scientists now believe the islanders helped bring about their own decline by manuring their fields with seabird carcasses. The soil still shows elevated levels of lead, zinc, cadmium, and arsenic from the birds.

Our world may be an example of what mathematicians call "the nut-room problem." It's impossible, they explain, to consume all the nuts in a closed room filled to the ceiling—at some point it becomes impossible to find the remaining kernels in a room full of shells.

CHAPTER 20

Goodbye, Mr. Shrdlu

An advancing Confederate brigade is said to have sacked the office of an abolitionist editor, then stuffed his type in a cannon and fired it down the street after him. It's hard to imagine what such fitting justice might be in the age of computerized typesetting, but the story is emblematic of what's happened to those of us who grew up toward the end of the Gutenberg type-on-paper era. As I flee up the street, away from modernity, I imagine being pursued by a barrage of quoin keys, Star rules, and pica poles, perhaps with a Ludlow machine or a Mergenthaler Linotype sailing by overhead.

The death of a technology is nothing new; who has a 5¼-inch floppy disk anymore, or a manual typewriter (besides me, that is)? But the end of type on paper—letterpress printing—was the passing of a culture that went back at least 500 years, and even further when one considers the Chinese. Not only machines changed, but also language, craftsmanship, jokes, and ways of thinking about the printed word. To have witnessed such a revolutionary change all the way through is, in its way, an honor, and I invoke the memoirist's privilege of telling about it.

One small measure of the change is that I never see my friend Etaoin Shrdlu in the newspaper anymore. To understand why requires knowing a little about the Linotype machine, Othmar Mergenthaler's 19th Century refinement on Gutenberg's moveable type. It was a large and complicated machine, though not as insanely so as the Paige typesetter, which had 18,000 parts and bankrupted Mark Twain.

Essentially, the Linotype was a small foundry. An operator at a keyboard could, with a touch, bring a brass matrix for a letter or punctuation mark hurtling down from a fan-shaped "magazine" that towered over the keyboard. When all the matrices for a "line o' type" had been assembled at the operator's left hand, he sent a stream of hot lead into the line to form raised letters on a lead "slug" that was exactly .918 of an inch high—"type high" the world over.

After the line was cast, a metal arm swung down, picked up the matrices, and returned them to the magazine, for use again. The operation was hot, noisy, and not without risk from hot slugs and squirting lead. But it also was a lot faster than an old-time printer assembling bits of type in a hand-held tray, or "stick."

Occasionally the Linotype operator realized that he had hit a wrong key, and that the line of type would have to be discarded. The quickest way to dispose of a bad line was to run one's hand down the left-hand keys, perhaps catching the space bar on the way. This produced a line reading "etaoin shrdlu," which inevitably got into print now and then to the puzzlement of readers. It has been a long time since I've seen the enigmatic Mr. Shrdlu's name in print. Young journalists look at you blankly if you mention him. Such knowledge is equivalent to using carbon paper, another antiquated technology that I cling to.

Twenty years ago, I could have bought a Linotype for next to nothing, but it would have required shoring up the house to support the machine's weight. Stick to stamp collecting, my wife suggested.

I felt the first tremor of the approaching revolution one day in 1956, when my typography class at the University of Missouri took a walk to the basement of another building on campus to see something that *looked* like a Linotype, but was labeled a Linofilm machine. The brass matrices still dropped, but each had a little window with a piece of film bearing a letter. As the matrices flew past, they were photographed on light-sensitive paper.

"In a few years, dirty old printers will be a thing of the past, and your newspapers will be put together by girls in white aprons," our instructor said. "Oh, sure," we thought.

But by the time I reached the Hornell *Evening Tribune* less than 10 years later, the revolution was under way. The *Trib* installed a Photon machine, a whirling drum with a light that picked letters off the circumference and transferred them to strips of paper. Jack, our mechanical foreman, went off to a training session in Boston, and returned to say that the instructors were so baffled by one aspect of the machine that its inventor was brought in from Vermont at great expense to tell them how to hook it up. Jack told us the inventor looked long and hard at his machine, and then said, "Oh, hell—hook it up one way, and if that doesn't work hook it up the other." That was my cue not to be awestricken by these strange new beasts.

Once the Photon was up and running, the *Trib* pensioned off its ancient Linotype operators and hired two young women, one of whom had been a waitress in a pizza parlor. They did just fine.

It was easier for small papers to change than for big ones, which had a fortune invested in the old technology. But while I was at the Louisville *Courier-Journal,* it also began revolutionizing production. For a while, we struggled with something called OCR—optical character recognition—a machine that scanned typewritten copy and (I believe) produced tape to drive the Linotype machines. This was a horrible idea, developed originally for classified-ad departments. Even if the reporter typed perfectly, we copyeditors still had to make all our changes and corrections with special pencils that the machine could read. A piece of copy could be so marked up that it was impossible to read by eye, even though the machine might set it perfectly. OCR died a quick death, at least in newsrooms.

The *Courier-Journal* got around the problems eventually by junking its Linotypes and going to a completely electronic system, with the reporters typing on terminals and the editors also doing their work there. Reporters and editors in effect became the typesetters, and all the old-time printers and proofreaders were let go. The savings, we were told, would provide vast amounts of money to improve newsroom operations and pay. We never saw it.

As we changed to this new system, my friend John Long was assigned to make it work, and he developed an eight-level tracking system to record changes in copy. Editors could mark deletions with a white highlight, additions with dark. Underlining meant something else, and there were additional ways to indicate editorial tinkering. The result, for heavily-edited copy, was a patchwork quilt on the screen that was almost as unreadable as OCR copy. We struggled bravely with it, until John noticed one day what we were doing. "All that was only supposed to be a training tool," he exclaimed. "I've created a crutch for a well man!"

Eventually, of course, the bugs were worked out. Dirty old printers disappeared entirely, and the girls in white aprons arrived—paste-up persons who cut up columns of "paper type" with X-acto knives and glued them onto the pages. These were then printed with the new "offset" presses that had replaced the old spinning lead plates. Karen was a PUP for a while, but began thinking of leaving one day when her supervisor stressed out on deadline and hurled an X-acto knife that barely missed a colleague's nose.

The paste-up era lasted a few years until the computer experts figured out how to lay out pages directly on a screen, once more putting the production responsibility on editors. The entire printing plate now can be made electronically, and plates themselves are being replaced on some publications by computerized ink jets that print directly onto newsprint. It is possible, at least experimentally, to update a story directly on the press during a printing run. The cry of "Stop the presses!" which was mostly a myth anyway, has joined the newsboy's "Wuxtra" in the gallery of superannuated language.

So where does that leave those of us who are somewhat superannuated ourselves? Actually in a pretty good position. Through the agencies of the laptop computer and its printer, I was able to format the pages you are reading, print out proofs, and download the whole book on a CD for the printer. This is print-on-demand publishing, with copies produced as they are ordered—no more ponderous inventory of unsold books.

A few years ago, in the *Peanuts* comic strip, Snoopy sent off his novel to the publisher, who replied: "We have sold one copy. When we sell another one, we'll print another copy." Which is exactly how POD publishing works.

Few technologies totally disappear. There are probably monks somewhere illuminating manuscripts, and I'm sure a Linotype is still clanking away, perhaps in a small printshop in East Overshoe, Mo. I treasure my Uncle Bill's 1923 Remington 16 manual typewriter, and type a lot of letters on it, using carbon paper to make copies. If the power goes off, I can stick a candle on the carriage and keep going.

Handset type and letterpress printing also keep right on going, but in the hands of artists now, who produce small editions of beautiful books. I correspond with one such artist, Jerry Reddan, at Tangram Press in Berkeley, Calif. Several years ago, Jerry was helping produce huge and expensive handset Bibles for the altars of huge and expensive churches. I expressed some interest, and Jerry sent me a prospectus with a sample page. The price, if I remember correctly, was $9,000 for an ordinary Bible and $12,000 for the deluxe edition.

"At that price," a friend said, "God should sign it."

A hand press in the Connor Museum of Antique Printing at Seymour, Indiana.

129

INTERVAL: TO THE AIRPORT!

Karen and I figured once that if we had gotten $25 for every run to the Indianapolis airport to pick up college visitors, I could have retired a year early. Editors, reporters, scholars, poets, conference speakers, job candidates—they all made the 27-mile trip with one or both of us, usually ending at a motel in Franklin. (I once lost a poet in the motel. The desk clerk wrote down the wrong room number, and neither of us had any idea where he was or how to find him.)

For a while, we counted airport runs, including personal ones, but we lost track after 400.

Usually we took visitors back to the airport, too. Karen holds the land speed record, with TV newsman Daniel Schorr. Dan was having a good time chatting at breakfast; she finally pried him away and made it to the plane in 33 minutes flat, with a stop for gas.

Helen Thomas of UPI, the doyenne of White House correspondents, rode with us. So did Walter Sullivan of the *New York Times* and Jim Polk of NBC News. But our favorites were not always big names. Susanna Rich, a writing teacher and textbook author, became a longtime friend, as did Marvin Sosna, a California editor.

The most fun among our passengers were probably Dave Lee, the "pig poet" of Utah, and a young Canadian author, Evelyn Lau. Dave, a superb poet who just likes to write about pigs, came as a result of a brainstorm with a faculty colleague. We put a number of related events together to make the college's first and only Pig Day. (This *is* Indiana, remember.)

Evelyn Lau had had a rough early life on the streets of Vancouver, and put her experiences into a best-selling diary. Over dinner with faculty, she told about her gritty life as a phone-sex operator. She had no sooner finished the story than a server arrived to tell us, in increasingly voluptuous terms, about the dessert menu. As he walked away, another teacher said to Evelyn, "You know, he could have had your old job."

It also amused Evelyn vastly that when she stopped to buy a bottle of wine at a Franklin liquor store, the clerk carded her.

CHAPTER 21

Journalsim

B ack in newspaper days, friends and I used to kid about the difference between "journalism"—competent, ethical—and "journalsim," everything else including the wrong, the vicious, and the silly.

At one point in writing this book, I produced a chapter giving a thoughtful analysis of the current state of the craft. "Throw it out," a wise editor urged. "It sounds pompous." And it was. I have no credentials as a pundit.

But after half a century in and around the subject, I can say, to news readers and viewers, use your good sense. Distinguish between journalism and journalsim. Respect and cherish the reporter who gets it right, who speaks carefully with a human voice. Tune out the one who says, "Millions of people believe . . . ." Has he counted them?

As I write this short chapter, after the rest of the book, terrorist bombs are going off. "Sense of dread descends on London," my morning paper exclaims. No, it hasn't. It didn't descend during the Blitz and probably not even, universally, during the Black Death. This is journalsim. I used to hype stories for UPI. I know.

A conservative friend recently proposed that journalists be licensed as professionals, under a national board of leading practitioners, with a federal overseer. I immediately proposed Karl Rove as the overseer, and my friend e-mailed back, "Did you say something? I wasn't listening." Alas, no one has proposed a workable way to allow free and responsible journalism while banning journalsim. Journalism is not, can never be, a profession, no matter how much its practitioners may lust for that status. In part, this is because it is a joint venture between reporters and readers/viewers. You, the audience, have the same basic skills and smarts as the journalist—be skeptical, use your own hard-earned knowledge of what is likely and of how the world works. Demand a second opinion. Be an informed consumer.

And if you really want to know what's going on, search out the journalists who are making that particular subject or corner of the world their specialty. A few months ago, a review led me to a book called *Black Garden*, by Thomas DeWaal, who has spent years visiting and thinking about the Caucasus and its sometimes deadly nationalisms. I read it with the wonderful sense of seeing a fine journalist at work.

When my Uncle Bill retired after 30 years as publications chief of the Bronx Zoo, he put animals away and went on to other things. I have done the same with journalism, although it is still a joy to work now and then with students. Their hopefulness is contagious. I still read newspapers, look at a little TV news (what I can stand), and even go to the internet now and then to check out the blogosphere. But I no longer need to follow every hurricane or terrorist attack in detail. I know what they are without needing multiple instances. So do you.

Years ago I used a commentary column from a newspaper to get this point across to journalism students whose minds were still dazzled by novelty. The column was titled, "I Never Read a Newspaper, and You Shouldn't Either." It ended by recounting the story of a coal miner trapped underground for six days in utter blackness. When interviewed after his rescue, he said he had done a lot of thinking down there and had come to a decision—he was going to cancel his newspaper subscription.

CHAPTER 22

The Canadian Student

Student-teacher friendships rarely last much beyond graduation. College slips into the past, and there are all those new freshmen. Yet there are exceptions. Karen and I still visit a former student every few years in England. There is the Brat Pack, three 40-somethings whom we meet for dinner once a month. There are occasional and Christmas correspondents, all valued. And there is Jen.

Jennifer Emily Olive Walters, from a small town on the central coast of Newfoundland, arrived at Franklin in the fall of 1991 as one of two exchange students from Acadia University in Nova Scotia. She and her companion, Penny Green, enrolled in my basic-reporting class, so for 14 weeks we saw each other four days a week, at 8 a.m. Jen and Penny easily outpaced their classmates, some of them barely awake at that hour. Jen was the second chair from the window in the second row—slender, dark-haired, wearing a simple yoked dress.

It wasn't a very memorable semester, although Jen and Penny came in one day with a mock-heroic tale of a photo assignment to a local mall. Someone had questioned their activities, and they peeled out of the parking lot just ahead of a police car, with Penny driving and Jen snapping pictures as they fled. Very uncharacteristic, since it's well known that Canadians are nicer than the rest of us and have no evil in their hearts.

The other thing I remembered later was Jen's way of crossing her eyes to indicate amazement at life's absurdity—her "I-can't-believe-it!" look.

Exchange students come and go. The Canadians took their As and headed home, soon to be forgotten—I thought. But then came a thank-you note from Jen (and for several years a Christmas card from Penny). I replied. Jen wrote back and at some point became a correspondent and a friend. It may have been when she sent Karen and me a box with bakeapple jam, Newfoundland hardtack, and a recipe for codfish stew, or "fisherman's brewis." "Here is what you must do," she prefaced the instructions.

In considering the paragraph above, I think this *was* the beginning—and that my life was different after that. I got deeply involved in Canadian Studies at the college, in part because I now had a friend in what she called, with self-mockery, "the Great White North." I wrote some poems because of stories she told me or phrases in her letters. I learned things, and one of them was that it was possible to care deeply for someone, with no shade of possessiveness.

Over the months and years, letters traveled back and forth as Jen and I went off to different parts of the world. After Acadia and a summer on her hometown paper, she began a master's degree in journalism at the University of Western Ontario. I was working in Taiwan by then, and when I reached my desk on the first day—full of qualms—a letter from Canada was waiting.

Jen finished her degree and described a rural visit with her sister, niece, and nephews. "My mom's scared for me," she wrote. "She figures I'm not safe in the country by myself . . . the university and 248 Steele Street are memories . . . our landlady became a tyrant, and we were visited by the police one morning. The result—a housemate was evicted as we, including him, stood in our nighties. Anyway, I'll tell you some other stories. Not now, as this is supposed to be an uplifting letter."

That last line typified what I came to think of as the Walters voice—direct, unabashed, with a twist of lemon at the end.

Fun to answer, too. "I can hardly wait to hear more about your sordid life on Steele Street," I replied. "You'll be fine in the country—it's the town that Mom should worry about."

I sent along, for the niece and nephews, a story I had written about a Chinese fairy and a despondent dragon whose tears kept putting out its fire. "Thanks so much for the story," Jen replied. "I had to read it—tried to save it for the nephews and niece, but really couldn't keep it in the envelope. . . . I love fairy tales, and the dragon tears were a wonderful touch. Ah, it makes my heart ache."

I returned to Franklin in the fall of 1994, and Jen spent several months in French immersion with a large and noisy Quebecois family. Her letters from that time show traces of 20-plus angst—career uncertainties, some family concerns, a romance that was nearing its end. But she recovered quickly, and went off to more French immersion near Avignon, where she described the furnishings of her apartment with a Gertrude Stein flair for verbal pizazz—"yellow lovely duvets!"

At the end of the program, she toured Ireland with her mother and aunt, in a group of older travelers who plainly had fallen for her. Afterward, left alone in Limerick on an interminable Irish Sunday, she wrote a long, thoughtful letter about the tour and her side trip through barbed-wire checkpoints into Belfast: "My eyes were opened," she said.

When Jen returned from Ireland, she seemed at loose ends for a while, doing short-term jobs and helping a family tear down a barn: "I loved the day and wished I could create a house of my own in a corner of their property—they'd never know I existed." Instead, she went to work for a Newfoundland newspaper and then a radio station, but these were not to her liking—nor was the fact that the reporters also had to deliver the papers. "I love digging up information and talking to people," she wrote, "but dislike the probing and invasion that often happen." Joining the communication arm of a nickel-mining company, she spent several months flying into Labrador villages on small planes to hold community hearings about a proposed mine and smelter. Her only requirement, she wrote, "was that the plane must have two engines."

FIVE-MOUNTAIN MORNING

I accused her in verse of not frolicking enough:

> *"Ask someone dangerous*
> *to tea," the poster said.*
> *That's my advice.*
>
> *Put down your pen and start*
> *this morning. Raise some hell*
> *and break some hearts.*

She promised to frolic more: "I seem to go through long periods of 'non' . . . and then *wham* it happens."

From nickel mining, Jen went to an agency planning a hydroelectric project at Churchill Falls in northern Labrador. She also began a long-distance MBA with a university in Victoria, British Columbia. Letters—and now e-mails—kept me abreast of her life and that of her family. I wrote about my own family, work, trips, college life, and news items I thought might amuse her—like an announcement of Gravity Observance Day: "I don't know what we're supposed to do to celebrate. Fall down, maybe." I also addressed her language questions, including the difference between "contented" (momentarily satisfied) and "content" (deeply and permanently happy). And Jen helped me translate some cryptic Canadian: "You can't get no double-double when you're turfed out on pogey."

"It means he can't afford a double-cream/double-sugar coffee because he's living on social assistance and that just won't cover it . . . poor bugger!"

Over the years, small gifts arrived from the North—an Irish saltspoon, maple and oak leaves from Newfoundland, commemorative coins, a folksong tape, and moose-related items. Moose became a theme in our correspondence after she sent a picture of a field full of them. "Hope the moose cheer up your end-of-summer blues," she wrote, and they did. Back from me went books, a Chinese penholder, and annual reminders of Little Burnt Bay Day, a minor Newfoundland fête that I managed to inflate to the importance of Victoria Day. Also an occasional job recommendation. (To an especially glowing one, she responded, "Jennifer WHO???")

Her letters drew me into an extended family that included not only her sister and children, but Mom, Aunt Mary, various uncles, and eventually even her Scottish brother-in-law's mother, with whom Karen and I spent a happy day near Inverness. The letters also told of her love for flowers, hiking, kayaking, cycling—anything to do with the outdoors. "My bike is my life," she wrote.

To my report of a rumor (unfounded) that Dan Rather would visit Franklin, she wrote that I should tip off the broadcasting students but give them very little time to react—"see how honed their skills are." "I can't believe it!" I replied. "Kindly Jennifer reveals herself as a media barracuda! How devious, how delightful!" To which she responded with the verbal equivalent of crossed eyes: "Devious? Never—never in a million years—well, maybe sometimes, yes . . . . Much love, the ever kindly, meek and mild Jen."

There was a marriage that ended after several years; Jen then moved all the way to Vancouver, where she finished her MBA and worked in communications for health agencies. At the university, she met Rick Hamilton, a savvy B.C. entrepreneur who had gone back to school to polish his business skills and had encountered his first Newfie. They went hiking and sat on a log, exchanging histories.

Long afterward she wrote, "I remember telling him about flying into Labrador on small twin engines, hoping my life would be spared . . . along with other tall tales. I can't remember what I told him!"

Jen and Rick were married in August, 2003. Would Karen and I come, and would I read a poem? Are there moose in Canada? Jen and Rick met us at the airport. I had a touch of first-date jitters—after all these years of correspondence, what if we didn't hit it off? But when Jen threw her arms around me, I knew everything would be all right.

The wedding was in the evening, on the terrace of the Vancouver Maritime Museum, with the lights of the city shining across the harbor. We had liked Rick at once; now we met Mom, Aunt Mary, Jen's sister Ann, and the legendary niece and nephews. I read the poem, which played on the transcontinental marriage and seafaring imagery. It ended:

> *. . . May the One who moves*
> *the stars and tides attend you on your way,*
> *bless and beguile your lives that here are blent,*
> *and bring us all, in fullness of our days,*
> *to continents of blessing, and content.*

Jen and Rick are now raising twin daughters, Paige and Sarah, and we are hearing all about it, from teething to a short-lived try at mother-baby yoga. "I started laughing," Jen wrote. She was in the back of the class, "looking at a sea of mommy's bums. Yep, it was absurd."

I could almost see her crossing her eyes.

Jen and Rick took Karen and me to lunch at the Bridges Restaurant next to Vancouver Harbor.

CHAPTER 23

Dreamland

K aren and I broke the lock on the castle gate and stormed inside with our band, vanquishing the defenders in a short but bloody fight. Then we sat down at a rough board table in the courtyard while an old man applied his code to our message. The numbers didn't match, the old man faded from view, and we knew that this time the combat had been a dream. We began preparing for the next battle.

This was dreamed (or double-dreamed) one afternoon while I was thinking about this chapter. As a writer, I pay attention to dreams for what they can tell me about reality, even though I know most of them proceed from Homer's deceitful gate of ivory rather than the true gate of burnished horn. At the worst (which is about 95 percent of the time), they are trivial and of interest only to the dreamer and his psychiatrist, who must be tempted to nod off at times. But the other five percent tell us something, often very directly, if we will listen. In one of them, I met the creative process itself. This was in Taipei, and I described the encounter to my son Mike, who was taking a writing class just then at the University of Kentucky:

> ". . . the hapless writer is trying to write and not having much success. Suddenly, the creative process enters. It is a large square, about eight feet on a side and a foot thick, garishly decorated and festooned with colored

lights. It looks something like the decorations here in Taipei for Double Ten Day. The square floats in the air like Ezekiel's chariot and gives forth raucous music, squawks, and garbled language. The author listens in frustration—but he does listen. And at last a gnomic figure pops up from the top of the square, utters the line the author was searching for, and disappears inside again. (Of course, I don't remember the line, but it was great.) So there you have it. That's what the creative process looks like and how it functions. You may want to inform the rest of your writing class. P.S. I was driving with friends in Taipei recently when we passed 'The Subconscious Café.' Someone said, 'I ate there once, but I can't remember anything about it.'"

Everyone has dreams, I believe, although the ability to recall them may atrophy from disuse. "I never dream," a new patient is supposed to have told Freud. "Don't worry, you will," the doctor replied. And Carl Jung once abandoned a case when his preliminary probing disclosed a personality so infantile that he feared the man would disintegrate under analysis. But these are extremes, and surely dreams are a resource available to most of us. The poet May Sarton said our writing sometimes is more mature than we are; dreams also can tell us about directions in which we are growing and even offer light along the way.

Sometimes the light is literal. In a dream, I set out for a destination, but the day darkened and at nightfall I found myself in a threatening neighborhood, but one I needed to cross. A man was making lamps nearby, and as I wrote later: "He offered to give me a lamp or rather make one for me, which he did by spinning acrylic glue around an acetylene torch. He explained that he had once gone to college but had learned that his professors were as ignorant as he was. So now he lived at the end of this street, constructing lamps for people who needed to go out across the waste of dark buildings."

The lampmaker was another of those helpful and encouraging dream figures like the gray-clad young woman who once brought me hot soup in the backyard of my grandparents' home. I'm grateful for these images and am not concerned about their source, or whether they are Jungian "animas" or poetic muses, although mine seem to be feminine more often than not.

Here is another helpful dream: I'm someplace in the country, where preparations are under way for an outdoor dinner. A cook gives me a basket and sends me up a little hill to "the old fruit barn" to collect some tomatoes. I find these but something else, too—a little hothouse garden with every sort of vegetable, common or exotic: radishes, parsnips, eggplant, carrots, salsify, kohlrabi, all growing in a rich mulch of straw in an old cold frame. I begin sampling and soon am eating voraciously. The last thing I try is a spearmint plant, which bears little pouches of sweet liquid, like white after-dinner mints. (So this is where they come from!)

Just describing the garden doesn't convey the richness of the place, the deep care with which all this has been planted and nurtured, apparently by a woman gardener who appears briefly. This surely is part of "the great good place" that exists somewhere for each of us—a memory of Eden. I gather some of the vegetables as well as the tomatoes and take them back in my basket. I am concerned not to take too much of anything, but nothing is depleted, although I have eaten like a sailor seeing fresh produce again after months at sea.

Most dreams are not this comforting. In many years of dream notation, I find several with inexplicable rage, some of it directed at my mother, something I wrote about in an earlier memoir. (My father usually is absent or passive in these.) This is hard for me to understand, since we seldom battled in life. Perhaps that itself is a reason for the dreams. Or maybe they are a residue of "Billy's temper tantrums" or of something even older. I wonder if a child born by Caesarean section after a prolonged labor has had an unsuccessful birth struggle that must be compensated for in some way? (As a child I could fly in dreams but lost that ability early.)

A fair number of my dreams involve buildings, often vast ones, with unsuspected rooms, galleries, and intersecting stairways—a Piranesi dreamscape. Sometimes I'm trying to repair these buildings, but find that the roof of one room has begun to leak again after I've moved on to the next. (I owned a house like that once, but the dreams go back farther.) Some dreams reflect, or perhaps are the cause of, my interest in "edge places." In late December, 1989, I was dreaming about islands off the coast of Ceylon (it was not Sri Lanka in the dream), just beyond the reach of those of us staying in a sort of 1910 beach spa. Several months later, the dream was repeated, this time with Venice as the locale. It took another 10 years for me to reach the actual islands, and then they were in the Scottish Hebrides.

Dreams sometime find their way into my poetry. One poem, "The New York Girl," begins in another fantastic house, and goes on to involve a girl I'm in love with, a murder, a hanged donkey, and the destruction of all the seats in a movie theater. It's too long to quote. It also exhibits a curious theatrical quality that shows up now and then in my unconscious imagining. In one dream, a mime performs "grave acts" and presentations, marking the end of each by bowing so that the top of his black stovepipe hat presents a period to the audience. In another, various avant garde performances take place, at the end of which the theater is torched, perhaps the ultimate plot device for an extremely limited engagement.

Fire figures more than once in these episodes. A locomotive burns up, also a school, and in another I imagine the first line of a short story: "The day began badly for Arthur Bartlett when his alarm clock caught fire." That's as far as I've gotten with the story. (Also, dear God, I find myself punning in dreams: "She wanted a house in a subdivision, but her husband was intractable.")

Dream people often have names I've never heard before, and detailed histories. Where, I wonder, is Fiona McLachlin, who helped me cover a plane crash next to the Manor restaurant in Franklin on the night of Jan. 22, 1995, and who was beaten by a crowd angry at journalists? And why does no biographical index contain the name of David Pope, 92, whose obituary I wrote during the night of Jan. 24, 1991? I know a lot about Pope, who was the thinnest man I had ever seen, so emaciated that there were actually holes all the way through his body, like a Henry Moore sculpture. I awoke feeling that he existed in some parallel universe.

I've forgotten what story went with a Feb. 21, 2000, entry: "Bad sex on a college campus from Hell." But I have what must be fairly ordinary anxiety dreams: realizing it's time for the final exam and I haven't been to class yet; being trapped in elevators ascending impossibly tall buildings; returning to previous jobs, sometimes more than once, in the hope that this time I'll get it right. I took a math test in a dream once, which I failed because I didn't know the name of an Arab who advised the king of Prussia on gunnery. If anyone knows the answer, please get in touch with me.

Dreams have also reflected deeper anxieties, including problems in speaking (difficult when one's mouth is full of ground glass) and in sustaining relationships. For many years I dreamed of meeting women and even being friends with them for long periods before thinking, "You know, we really ought to get married." After a few years of marriage to Karen, she subtly worked her way into these dreams, so that she was the one I was considering. And in recent years, there has been a further advance on my part to, "Oh, we *are* married." I'm sometimes a little slow to catch on, but I get there eventually.

Some dreams have involved unlikely family scenes. My son Colin and I spent the night of Dec. 10, 1990, calling on Uncle Dudley Hunter, my great-grandmother's brother, whom I never met in life but who was still living in a nursing home in dreamland, at the age of about 150. "Well, I'll be damned!" he greeted us, an understandable reaction under the circumstances. I also hold to an immensely comforting dream, in which my closest relatives—my parents Eve and Jack, my uncles, my grandfather Harry—have returned to the kitchen of the family home on Yandes Street in Franklin. My father has baked Boston brown bread in a tin can, something he often did there. Everyone is talking comfortably, and I am with them, a part of the circle. I awoke with the feeling, familiar to other dreamers, that this had been the reality and that nothing and no one had been lost, whatever calendars and tombstones might say.

What other dreams mean, or which gate they came in by, remains a profound mystery to me, on which I do not care to be enlightened. How did I get to be a member of a gang of thugs, looting gold and gems from the ruins and rubbish heaps of a vast post-Roman city, until we were deliberately poisoned by broth served to us in alabaster dishes shaped like fish? There's a novel in there if I could find it.

Dreams can change with time. My animas and muses seem to be aging along with me, which I think I'm happy about. One of them left me in November, 2001, for a new love, a young guy just out of prison. "But you're still my oldest boy-friend," she said. "If there were any older ones, I'd feel sorry for you," I replied. By this time I had already met Retha, a beautiful though fragile older woman whose home I visited on the evening of Oct. 31, 1997:

> *Some dreams we want*
> *to return to, they had so much*
> *to tell us, such deep resonance—*
> *the woman in that house*
> *of thoughtful objects,*
> *who was frail and wise,*
> *and how we walked later*
> *along a shaded street,*
> *and I picked up a stone*
> *for memory . . .*

Dreams for me are often intimately connected with the idea of home. I once went with my father to visit *his* father's boyhood home in the country near Franklin. This was the house from which my grandfather Harry set out for school on winter mornings with the warm potatoes his mother had put in his pockets. The house meant little to me and the owner was gone, so we couldn't see inside except by peering through the lace curtains, which of course we did. But my father spoke warmly about his boyhood visits there, and how a scythe had been left hanging in a tree until the tree had grown round and captured it. His eyes were bright with recollection, and he was seeing—in a waking dream—the family and friends he had loved.

While writing this, I revisited in a dream another kind of home, a place I have been often and know well, although it does not exist in our time or space. In my dream, it always seems to be connected in some way with my old college, although its existence has been forgotten for many years. Its main feature is an old-fashioned building, not large but three stories tall, with a cupola. There does not seem to be much inside the building, but there are windows on all sides of the rooms—through-lights to use an old term. It is a building designed to be looked out of, and what the rooms are full of is not furniture but light.

INTERVAL: DETOUR

Dear Amanda and Mike:

We want you to know that we obtained this beautiful cherry footstool as a wedding present for you under considerable difficulties. The footstool was at The Sampler, a cherry-furniture store in Homer, Indiana. We were in Franklin. Between us and the footstool was extensive construction on State Road 44, requiring back-road detours into parts of Indiana only rarely seen by anyone not named Clyde or Leroy. We begin this account at the turnoff from 44 toward the community of Bengal, with Karen driving.

Karen: I wonder if they have tigers.

Bill: You may rest assured that if there were a high school, teams would be known as the Bengal Tigers.

Karen: Wow, look at that corn! I've never seen corn so green.

Bill: Nor have I, and look, here we are at the Bengal Christian Church, which has a full-size replica of the Liberty Bell in the yard. Let's turn left and remember the bell, so we can find our way back.

Karen: The road is getting narrower. But I see another car in the distance. We're not alone.

Bill: No indeed, and if you'll turn right at that big, shiny grain bin, we should soon be in the metropolis of Marietta.

Karen: Oh, yes, there it is. My goodness, it has a volunteer fire department.

Bill: And a fish fry every month. A thriving city, although you can still see cornfields in all directions.

Karen: I believe we're on the road to Smithland now. Would you look at that corn! It's even greener than the last field.

Bill: And the soybeans are greener, too. Wow! We must be in the fabled Vale of the Calmuck, where the crops are more bountiful and the livestock fatter than anywhere else. By the way, dear, would you mind driving closer to the center line?

Karen: Why? I've got plenty of room.

Bill: Because, my light of love, I am considerably nearer the edge of the road than you, and am looking straight down into a six-foot bar ditch.

Karen: Oh. Well, close your eyes. That's what I'm doing.

Bill: This crossroads must be Smithland. Yes, there's a pole barn with a sign: "The Smithland Apartments." It sounds positively urban.

Karen: Look, there's more corn, and it's really tall.

Bill: Look at the corn on my side. It's even taller than on yours.

Karen: You moron, that's because it's on a hill.

And so on and on and on.

We eventually reached Homer, collected the footstool, and returned to Franklin, only 19 hours after setting out on what is ordinarily a 45-minute trip. We hope you are properly appreciative.

Your loving parental units.

Photo by Dennis Cripe

At a 2003 retirement dinner in the Franklin College Campus Center. Seated from left: Amber Baldwin, Karen Bridges, Bill Bridges, and Rebecca Bridges. Standing: Amanda Baldwin and Michael Bridges, who were married later in the year; Rita Cates Bridges and Karl Bridges; Colin Bridges; David Bridges and Connie Godwin Bridges.

CHAPTER 24

Monkey Man

September 11, 2001, overwhelmed my skepticism about politics and political leaders. Sometime on that dreadful day, I wrote a short (and unpublished) column of reaction. "I was a child in World War II, and it feels like war to me today," it began. "We will do our work and live our lives, but on a war footing from now on, just as people did during the Blitz or as people do every day in parts of the world where terrorism is a daily fact. President Bush, not always my favorite, set the right tone of dogged persistence."

But the attitude of those words, and the willingness to have faith in political leaders, didn't last. In a very few months, well under a year, the drums were beating for war against Iraq and Saddam Hussein. Something had happened, and the terrorists who brought down the World Trade Center were no longer the chief enemy.

In late summer of 2002, a friend mentioned that he had been reading Edward Gibbon's 18th Century classic, *The Decline and Fall of the Roman Empire*, and had come across "a passage dealing with the Emperor Julian in 363 A.D. He was east of Baghdad with his Roman legions, anticipating a conquest of Persia. Unfortunately, the Persians conducted a scorched-earth policy, which trapped Julian far from his food supplies. Then the Persians turned loose their cavalry and elephants on the trapped legions, killing the emperor and slaughtering his soldiers."

I took down my own dusty two-volume set of Gibbon, and—half as a joke—told a writing friend on the East Coast that we should read our way through it, at 10 pages a day. "Nobody now alive has ever made it to Volume II," I told her. The friend (I'll call her Stella) grabbed her own copy of Gibbon and wrote back, "Dahlink, isn't this fun? I'd read the Monkey Man if he were writing a manual on furnace repair."

Thus began a curious several months in which Gibbon, the buildup to the Iraq war, and our e-mails to each other created a sort of running commentary on the times. So much has happened since (is still happening) that it's difficult to remember those months—Washington's insistence, with utter certainty, that Iraq had weapons of mass destruction, the deliberations in the U.N., the return of weapons inspectors to Iraq, the House resolution of Oct. 11, 2002, allowing the president to use military force if the U.N. failed to act.

Stella and I didn't limit our e-mail conversation to current events. In fact Gibbon proved entertaining for many reasons. I enjoyed reporting to her (she is also a teacher) that "Gibbon says the Emperor Maximin was eight feet tall, could move a loaded wagon, break a horse's leg with his fist, crumple stones in his hand, and tear up small trees by the roots. That should meet all the search committee's requirements."

But Gibbon also sounded eerily modern at times: "The arts of Severus cannot be justified by the most ample privileges of state reason. He promised only to betray, he flattered only to ruin; and however he might occasionally bind himself by oaths and treaties, his conscience, always obsequious to his interest, always released him from the inconvenient obligation."

"Gibbon is wonderful, isn't he?" I wrote to Stella. "I've gone on to the doomed effort of Severus to conquer the Scots, who kept escaping over the mountains like Bonnie Prince Charlie. And there are his observations that 'chastity was very far from being the most conspicuous virtue of the Empress Julia' and that 'luxurious entertainments, midnight dances, and licentious spectacles present at once temptation and opportunity to female frailty.' (Just wanted to see if you were still reading.)"

"Yes, dear sexist piglet," she responded, "but I'm falling behind in Gibbon. Are coffee breaks and some skimming allowed?"

In early December, 2002, Deputy Defense Secretary Paul Wolfowitz was saying that the U.S. would not act unilaterally even if Iraq failed to honestly declare its weapons of mass destruction. Gibbon was describing Diocletian ("Profound dissimulation under the guise of military frankness") and calling the Roman Senate "a venerable but useless monument of antiquity on the Capitoline Hill."

"The events are in themselves both interesting and important," he continued, "but still more as they contributed to the decline of the empire by the expense of blood and treasure, and by the perpetual increase, as well of the taxes as of the military establishment."

On Dec. 21, I was suggesting that we suspend Gibbon at Chapter 15 while Karen and I were on a Caribbean trip. "We'll be on a couple of islands, including one with an active volcano. Want to come along? We could be a joint sacrifice."

"Thanks, dahlink," Stella replied, "but I think the Volcano God requires teen-age virgins. I'm glad your Gibbon is in suspenders at Chapter 15, as is mine. This is more work than I thought, and lots else is going on. Could you give me updates?"

On Jan. 2, 2003, Defense Secretary Donald Rumsfeld authorized deploying thousands of troops to the Middle East.

On Jan. 30, I was writing, "Stell, you will be interested in Sopor's siege of Nisibis, a city in or near present-day Iraq, during which the Persian general dammed a river and created a lake, from which his troops battled the Roman defenders of the local castle at parapet height, until a wall collapsed, involving both sides in a sea of mud and elephants. Another Gibbon giblet: a new word, 'pravity.' It means the same as 'depravity' and will be useful in Scrabble (seven letters that everyone will challenge). Don't miss G's description of the Hippodrome and the spiral staircase that was known as the Cochlea—I'll never think of my inner ear the same way again. That's all of *Bill's Notes*. If you can't pass the test with those, I give up."

Stella replied, "I'm just back from the supermarket, where a tabloid screamed at me: "Saddam goes into exile—in New Jersey!" Am checking out the new neighbors."

On Feb. 6, 2003, Secretary of State Colin Powell was presenting "irrefutable and undeniable" evidence to the U.N. of Iraqi weapons of mass destruction. Two days later, Stella wrote, "Times get scarier, now that Germany, France, and even Brave Little Belgium are coming out against us. Maybe there's hope, though, if enough old friends desert us."

I described for her a war protest which "went off well, with a packed room and probably 50 poets reading. The art museum finally kicked us out about 10:30 p.m. There was a lot of good stuff: among my favorites, a poem explaining (with visual aids) a system of color-coded national shame alerts."

About this time, another e-mail correspondent sent along a website notice: "These weapons of mass destruction cannot be displayed. The weapons you are looking for are currently unavailable. The country might be experiencing technical difficulties, or you may need to adjust your weapons inspection mandate."

The same correspondent also proposed creation of the Ostrich Society, which would recognize that "the real problem with the War on Terror is that it will erode basic concepts of decent and civil behavior. Members of the society, like medieval monks, will serve civilization by keeping these basic tenets alive, ready to be reintroduced at some better future time. Have good manners and treat the people you come in contact with nicely. Don't encourage the politicians and terrorists by paying attention to them." The writer also proposed "Ostrich Alerts":

```
    ____!!____              !!
        !!                  !!
        !!                  !!
        !!              ____!!____
        !!                  !!
        O>                  O>
   Highest Alert        Lowest Alert
```

Gibbon continued to sound up to date: "The hardy [Roman] veterans, accustomed to the cold climate of Gaul and Germany, fainted under the sultry heat of an Assyrian summer; and the progress of the army was exhausted by the incessant repetition of a slow and dangerous retreat in the presence of an active enemy."

In March, I was catching Stella up with other Gibbon items. "Thirty ecclesiastics burned up in a ship, perhaps accidentally. Saxons strangled themselves rather than submit (is this possible?). Arsaces, king of Armenia, was locked in the Castle of Oblivion with the stuffed skin of his favorite general. Cannibals were alleged to have existed where Glasgow now stands. The Roman Empire continued to decline."

In mid-March, the U.N. secretary general warned the U.S. it would be in breach of the U.N. Charter if it attacked Iraq without Security Council approval.

"May you have love and peace in your house in this difficult time," Stella wrote.

On March 20, just before dawn, air-raid sirens in Baghdad announced the beginning of the war.

On April 14, 2003, I wrote Stella: "I am enjoying a respite from our learned friend, having completed the first volume of the *Decline and Fall*. The problem with decline-and-fall books is that things never get any better. They're a little like U.S. foreign policy. Oh, they may pick up briefly with a reforming emperor, but you know he's doomed.

"It all gets depressing after a while, and I'd quit except that I've taken the Vow. But I don't know if I have the stamina to begin Volume II, and if I made it through Volume II would I then be like Alaric, of whom my encyclopedia says: 'His work [the sack of Rome] being done, his fated task, nothing remained for him but to die.'?

"There have been some Gibbon gems in the last few chapters: his superb description of the camp of Attila the Hun, his mini-bio of St. John Chrysostom, and his tale of the empress who returned from Jerusalem 'with the chains of St. Peter, the right arm of St. Stephen, and the undoubted picture of the Virgin, painted by St. Luke.'

"Gibbon even has a word to say on the invasion of Iraq: 'Experience has shown that the success of an invader most commonly depends on the vigor and celerity of his operations.' Alas, it also depends on having some idea of what to do with the conquered country, and we don't seem to have much of one. I suspect this is just the beginning."

CHAPTER 25

A Month in Siberia

Were it not for Olga, I wouldn't know that an *oblam* is the second tier of a medieval Russian log fortress, or *ostrog*. Or that the world's oldest newspaper may be the *Ustyug Chronicler*, which began in a Siberian church in the 13th Century and ended only in 1950.

Olga entered my life in early December, 2004, when I was looking for a little free-lance editing to defray the cost overrun on a new front porch. She was trolling for English-speaking editors, and I took the bait. Glancing carelessly at her e-mail, I saw *.msu* and thought Michigan State University. It was Moscow State and I had casually signed on to help edit the English version of an "encyclopedia of peoples of the North." Or as the project's unusual abbreviation plan might have put it, "an encyc. of p. of N." There was a rudimentary style guide, written partly in Russian, which I do not read or speak. One American editor, whose reply to Olga crossed my computer, had already run screaming from the room.

What a wimp. I've always thought a professional editor should be able to work on anything from a railway timetable to *War and Peace*, but this belief was about to be tested. The next month would be among the most intense, interesting, frustrating, and (at times) most fun in a long life of editing.

Olga dangled fairly tasty bait. Editors would be paid $5 for every 1,800 characters, including spaces. A quick calculation turned this into $5 a manuscript page—$20 an hour, maybe more, for a fast editor. Editing standards didn't seem terribly demanding; the project was being done quickly, and I would be able to zip along. The deadline to finish the book was Dec. 22-23, two weeks away. If I worked steadily and didn't sleep much, I could grab enough of it to knock off some porch pain.

Over the next 11 days, I worked 104 hours and plowed through 249 pages. The letter U, a section of Y, and part of K disappeared in my wake. K was a monster, weighing in at 241 pages—there are enough Ks in Russian to stretch from Kiev to Kamchatka, with side trips to Krasnoyarsk and the Kuril Islands. One day I put in 14½ hours in the upstairs study that became known as Siberia, the tundra, and sometimes the gulag. While toiling thorough an entry on serfdom, it occurred to me that I was becoming something of an electronic serf myself. "Well, of course!" someone said delightedly. "You're serfing the internet!"

There were delicious moments, though. "The Russian Army fired martyrs at the oncoming troops," one translator wrote. Get those bearded guys into the cannons! August in the Kurils is sunny, wrote another, "except for the occasional onslaught of tycoons." I hadn't been so tempted to let errors stand since an academic colleague wrote that he had "traveled wildly in many parts of the world."

The Russian translators did just what my young Chinese reporters had done when I edited for the *Free China Journal* in Taiwan. When stumped for an English equivalent, they consulted their Russian-English dictionaries and often chose the most obscure equivalent. Thus, when the Russian writer spoke of "furuncles," I had to back-translate to find that these were simply boils.

Some entries were well-written and intriguing. The one on wooden forts was a joy, as were those on polar exploration and Admiral Kolchak's ill-starred White Russian republic. Olga played it straight politically, although she confessed in an e-mail that she had to struggle with a few unreconstructed Communists among her authors.

Balancing the "good" entries were scores—hundreds!—of mini-biographies of authors and artists, which told almost nothing about them except the titles of their books and the exhibitions in which their work had appeared. (My favorite exhibition: "We Are Building the BAM," or Baikal-Amur Mainline, an unfortunate acronym for a railroad.) And there were endless, if valuable, articles on native peoples of northern Asia. After slogging through eight or 10 pages of one, I learned there were fewer than two dozen of the tribe left. But none of these articles matched for tedium a 15-page piece capsulizing the holdings of every regional archive in Russia, with all their name changes since the 1917 Revolution.

Meanwhile, Dec. 22-23 came and went. Olga said she had enough edited copy to keep the printers at bay, and would I stay on? Of course. I packed up my laptop and took it along to a family Christmas in Virginia, where my daughter-in-law stoked the coffee pot so I could turn it on and edit at 4 a.m.

Olga's good humor and lavish praise, and my growing pile of rubles, kept me at it. "It is very important for me to feel that at least part of this book is being edited by a real professional," she wrote. And later, "Bill, you ARE a treasure." We argued occasionally, the first time over her determination to preface any approximate number with a "*c.*" but no following space. "Please, do not touch our beloved *circas*," she wrote. I questioned whether "BUGS" was an appropriately scientific entry title, but didn't get anywhere. More seriously, I tried to get Olga to adopt Inuit for Eskimo throughout the circumpolar region. (In Canada, at least, Eskimo is derogatory.) She gave in, sort of, on Canada, but said "Eskimo" is what this Siberian people calls itself. (Does it? I had trouble imagining little Nanook calling himself by the English word "Eskimo." But the chief editor is boss, and "Eskimo" it remained.)

My plan to zip through 10 pages an hour was breaking down. It took time to enforce some order on an abbreviation system that threatened to make the text unreadable if not uneditable. Would anyone decipher "The mus. exh. incl. hist. settl. sit. on Kizhi Isl."? Would anyone even try? I rebelled only at "smts" for "sometimes," and Olga let me win that one. All this truncating was to save space and money, but I could occasionally sneak full words back in by compressing some wordy writing elsewhere. That effort drew a thank-you from Olga's colleague, Natasha, in Sevastopol, who apologized for writing. "Usually, I just sit here within the text," she said—a good place for editors.

I also found I couldn't just copyedit obviously wrong statements and let them pass. I got Olga to back off a researcher's insistence that F.W. Cook rather than Robert Peary had discovered the North Pole. There's still a smouldering argument about that, but most sources give the nod to Peary. The names of polar explorers gave the translators a lot of trouble. Peary became Piri, William S. Laughlin turned up as U.S. Laflin, and the Canadian William Moor was found masquerading as the curiously oriental U. Mur, aboard a ship that had become the *St. Rock* instead of the *St. Roch*. I ransacked the internet to track down the correct names, although the best source for these turned out to be my 1911 *Encyclopaedia Britannica*.

There were other challenges that only another editor would recognize or care about. Maintaining some consistency of style was one, as was coping with the translators' habit of punctuating long lists with dashes instead of rational semicolons and colons. I had to diagram some passages, especially in the folklore entries, to make sure that tribal implements and clothing went with the right tribes.

The entries arrived in groups alphabetized by the Russian of the original text. By early January, Olga was pulling out groups of entries and slamming them into sections arranged by the English alphabet, at a rate of two letters a day. For one day we worked together in real time as she fired short sections over the internet and I fired them back edited. I took on a new job, checking entry titles and hyperlinks against a master word list or *slovnik*. (I knew I was deeply into this when I began learning the Cyrillic alphabet.)

Then it was done, 34 days (with one day off) from the start. I had edited 804 manuscript pages of highly condensed copy, spent a total of 249 hours (or almost eight hours a day), exchanged about 100 (sorry, *c*.100) e-mails with Olga, and ripped through 1,676,607 characters and spaces, about a fifth of the finished book. At the pay formula, that worked out to $4,657.24 or about $16 an hour—well under my usual asking price, but pretty close to my usual getting one. And what else would I have been doing, except watching the hapless Indiana Pacers and falling into depression? I spent an average of 18.6 minutes on each page, but this included research and e-mail time as well as the editing itself.

I don't know if I'll ever see a copy of the finished encyclopedia, and it doesn't matter. Editors move on. I have a few doubts about the book's utility, but it does make available to western researchers some information they could otherwise find only in Russian, at a monastery in Yakutsk.

The project gave me something worthwhile, though, besides pay and an exhaustive knowledge of North Russian subjects beginning with U, Y, K, and parts of L, A, and G. It showed me I could still do industrial editing. Partway through the project, I learned that I'd passed the test to do contract editing for an Indianapolis firm that publishes the "for Dummies" books. But I was nearly brain-dead. I had to stop myself from abbreviating ordinary words in letters and speech. I developed an ache in my left side and checked with my doctor to see if stress was doing me in. Not at all, he said—it's just a normal ache of the aging. My blood pressure was fine, and I apparently was thriving, as always, on deadlines.

But I also realized that I'd been on a manic high for more than a month and didn't really want to do this again, or at least not with the same intensity. I wanted my life back. When the time comes to remodel the bathroom, I think I'll take out a loan.

A FOOTNOTE ON COPYEDITORS

In a little book titled *Dear Viola*, I tried to capture the essence of this odd profession. Here it is, adapted:

A good editor is the one whose hand was always waving in English class. She reads a lot, enjoys playing with language and has a retentive memory. Spelling and grammar are seldom a problem, and when they are, she knows her way to the dictionary and stylebook. Most of all, she enjoys making the writing of others better, and is happy to let the writers take the credit. Copyeditors almost never get bylines.

After a few years as an editor, she will not be able to read anything purely for pleasure; her eye will go instantly to the misspelled *recieve* halfway down the page.

A good editor spends a lifetime stocking her mental attic with information she may never use. She knows there is no period in Dr Pepper, that Fels Naptha soap misspells naphtha, and that from anywhere in El Salvador one can see a volcano. She has a dogged determination to keep her publication up to the mark, even when it means correcting the same mistakes day after day, year after year. "The thrill of monotony," editing guru John Bremner called it.

I heard once that editions of Plato use a unique line-numbering system. Being a copyeditor, I couldn't leave this alone, and put out a call for help to a nationwide copyeditors listserv. One answer came back, from a woman named Alice, who explained that texts of Plato use "Stephanos numbers," which go back to the printer who created the system in the 16th Century.

I don't know who or where Alice is, but she's my kind of woman.

CHAPTER 26

The Cat of Pure Being

Something would be missing in these memoirs without some mention of the animals we have lived with. There have been a lot of them—hamsters, gerbils, fish, a few dogs, and a guinea pig who learned to associate the opening of the refrigerator door in the next room with the imminent arrival of lettuce.

But in recent years, most of our housemates have been cats. They make more sense for city dwellers. To avoid enraging any readers, I'll stop short of saying they are more intelligent than dogs, and will simply pass on someone else's question: "Did you ever hear of nine cats pulling a sled?"

I've always been intrigued that cats do not meow at each other, only at people. Dogs bark for the hell of it, at anybody and anything. Cats make the effort to speak our language.

Aside from that, cats differ wildly in their personalities and attractions. And in their problems: we have one at the moment who thinks outside the box and is undergoing aromatherapy for this. But I don't want to stretch readers' patience by going on about all of them. Instead, here is a short story I wrote, about one whose name actually was Blackie and with whom I had a close relationship. When I sent tapes back from Taiwan, Blackie would come thundering (the right word) from wherever he was to the tape recorder. There he would look at Karen in frustrated disgust: "You've got him in that black box—let him out!"

The story was written as fiction, but except for the *denouement* and the main character's name, it is almost 100 percent fact.

THE CAT OF PURE BEING

In *Henderson, the Rain King*, Saul Bellow writes, "I have never seen any member of the cat species pass through a door except on its own terms."

Anyone who has ever belonged to a cat knows the truth of this. When I read it, I thought of one cat whose terms were . . . . but let me start at the beginning, B.C., Before Cat.

I think we had known for a long time that something was circling us, advancing warily from the garden, to the garage, and finally to the front porch. My wife went out one morning to get the paper and left the door open. When she returned, he was crouched in the center of the living room—a black mountain of truculent tomcat, who had made it into the house at last and was not about to leave.

"Shoo!" my wife said. He wouldn't shoo. He was too big to throw out, and there was the question of claws. So she left the job for me, which was a mistake. The moment this cat and I saw each other, we were soulmates.

"You keep him, you name him," my wife said.

Something told me not to dally over a name or saddle him with one he would have trouble living up to. "No problem," I said. "His name is Cat."

Cat settled down to domestic life with his people and three spayed females who disdained him. It developed that he had some peculiar habits. He could not mew or purr; instead, he produced grunts, adenoidal snores, a sound like pigeons cooing, and long, lacerating laments, wrung from his soul at 3 a.m. as he kneaded his way over my wife and me in our bed. He also stank, with a vile essence of tomcat that might have made him

162

popular in a dump or an alley but did nothing to ease his entry into polite society.

My wife didn't exactly say "it's him or me," but I got the idea. Cat went out the door in the only way he was ever to go out a door again—in a carrier, to the vet, for alterations that would make him socially acceptable in a house of females and furniture.

I saw a cartoon once of a cat draped limply over the back of a sofa. "He's been neutered, deodorized, declawed, and de-fanged," his owner is saying. "He thinks he's a doily."

In his changed condition, Cat found his true doily na-ture—not to do but to be. Relieved of the painful burden of sex, he was a new and happier male. No more truculence, no lamen-tations at 3 a.m., and best of all no smell. The other cats began to accept him in the same way, I imagine, that the sultan's harem might have accepted an especially fat and foolish eunuch.

This is all anthropomorphic nonsense, of course. Who knows what cats think? But at least Boots, Ashley, and Polly stopped hissing at Cat and began pushing him away from the food dish with impunity. Cat took this calmly—he was either a perfect gentleman or an utter wimp. He got his time in later at the dish and soon began to take on the size, shape, and solidity of a small steamer trunk.

Watching the other cats, he learned about litter boxes, hearths, and scratches behind the ears. On his own, he learned about being locked accidentally in the attic—the only time he ever uttered anything like the despairing cries of his pre-vet days. The one thing he would not do, even briefly, was go through any door that led outside.

For one night, he became a party animal. Our guests dis-covered that, if they stroked Cat's back just forward of his tail, he would lick a particular spot on his right shoulder. Everyone was fascinated with this demonstration of applied neurology, and I had to put a stop to it while Cat still had shoulder fur.

When spring came, the other cats went for outings in the yard, but Cat refused to leave the house. No temptation—the food dish moved to the back step, the sight of finches at the feeder—would persuade him that he had lost anything out there worth going back for. He had become House Cat.

And not just House Cat, but House Cat on his way from what Bellow describes as the state of Becoming to the state of pure Being. He began viewing us with a serene and sorrowful gaze. He lived quietly, offering no offense and suffering meekly the offenses of others. Polly, a neurotic with wild mood swings, would leap from my wife's arms and head straight to slap Cat, but Cat never slapped back. At most, he cringed slightly when he saw her flying toward him.

His habitual expression—if a cat can have such a thing—was of gentle perplexity, tempered by trust that somehow all would be well. He began sleeping in the "dead-cat" position, with all four feet in the air, belly exposed and vulnerable. At other times he meatloafed in the center of the house traffic pattern with the immobility of a Buddha. If he ever glanced out an open door, it was only to view the world beyond as a place of cold, rain, and hunger—the *maya* of existence before The House.

Cat didn't forget his special relationship with me. Whenever I headed for the bedroom, he was there first, sprawled on the quilt, ready for a little sack time *a deux* with his person. Bellow notes that people come to resemble their animals; I grew more placid, put on weight, and began writing Taoist verse.

Then one day a crisis arose. A new job opened for me, necessitating a move to an apartment far away. The house went up for sale, and new homes had to be found for the animals. Rooms were emptied of furniture, books, food dishes, and litter boxes.

When it was time to load Cat for the trip to his new home with my sister, he was nowhere in sight. We searched the nearly empty house and garage, tramped through the garden, looked under the hood of the car, questioned the neighbors. No Cat.

The new homeowner was coming. There was nothing to do but lock up and go.

A few days later, the new owner called. "Are you missing someone?" he asked. "When I got here and opened up, this enormous black animal was crouched in the middle of the living room."

Find your own explanation. I believe that while we were searching frantically for him, Cat had finally passed though the door of pure, incorporeal Being. I had been found wanting, and we were no longer soulmates. I had lost him to the more powerful union of house cat and house.

"We seem to have hit it off," the new owner said. "If you want, I can keep him. But how do I get him to go outdoors?"

INTERVAL: E-MAIL
(or why secretaries leave home)

Place: Pulliam School of Journalism, Shirk Hall

Time: About 11 a.m. on a Tuesday. We are communicating by e-mail although our offices are next door to each other.

Arliene: It's time to order your lunch for the departmental lunch meeting. What sandwich would you like from Subway?

Me: A roast-beef sandwich, medium rare.

Arliene: What kind of chips do you want?

Me: Potato.

Arliene: No, I mean what style?

Me: [After reflective pause] Ruffles, with the ridges exactly two centimeters apart and no more than .005 of a gram of salt per chip.

Arliene: The rest of the department is ordering ridges one centimeter apart. Why are you different?

Me: It's because I'm more broad-minded than the others.

Arliene: Oh, puh-leeze!

[Half an hour goes by.]

Arliene: What kind of bread do you want on your sandwich?

Me: A delicate brioche, with just a hint of hazelnut.

Arliene: Now cut that out!

CHAPTER 27

A Little Late Pear Wine

As I approached retirement from Franklin College, certain comments came more frequently: (to me) "You'll be busier than ever," and (to Karen), "He'll drive you crazy." Since neither of these outcomes was one we wanted, there was some serious discussion of how to avoid them.

Being "busier than ever" was a dire thought. While certain job pressures had eased after my return from Taiwan in 1994, the subsequent years were quite busy enough. I had continued teaching journalism and critiquing the school paper; the two-page weekly critique eventually turned into a book, *Dear Viola: Reporting, Writing, and Editing for the Student Journalist.* I also took on directing the college's Canadian Studies program, and continued organizing conferences and visits by journalists and others.

For several years I taught in the college's freshman remedial-writing program, which taught me things about writing and about myself as a teacher. At the normal retirement age of 65, the college let me create and occupy a new position as director of the Pulliam School of Journalism, which now had a faculty and staff of eight and 180 majors. I was to organize the job over two years, then retire and turn it over to someone else. Busier than ever in retirement? No, thank you.

"But you'll continue teaching some classes, won't you?" was another frequent question. The answer was no; retirement is called that for a reason. I took myself off the college's e-mail, which amazed the Computer Center—apparently no retiree had ever requested a cutoff before, but I had seen enough faculty messages and bookstore-sale announcements. A colleague kindly forwards anything she thinks I really need to know.

Karen was irritated a bit by the assumption that, without anything to do, I would be underfoot and telling her how to run the household. "I still know how to go to the grocery by myself," she said. We hadn't had such problems in 40 years; why should they begin now? A couple of journalists should be able to write a better story.

Several months before retirement, we went to St. Maarten in the Caribbean for our 40th wedding anniversary, but on our own without benefit of cruise ship or packaged tour. And, gee, since we were in the neighborhood and liked islands, why not hop over to Antigua? And (gee again) Antigua was only 30 miles from a very live volcano on Montserrat—how could journalists pass up such a chance? A helicopter flew us almost to the crater rim, and we later spent a couple of days on the island, waking in the morning with volcanic ash between our teeth.

Other things were happening to take one's mind off retirement. In the fall of 2002, President Bush was beginning to push hard for action against Saddam Hussein in Iraq. Out in Port Townsend, Wash., poet and publisher Sam Hamill, who had visited Franklin a few months before, was organizing "Poets Against the War," which eventually drew contributions from more than 13,000 writers. I sent in an anti-war poem, and also read during an evening of protest at the Indianapolis Art Museum.

But the calendar was sliding by. Karen would go on reporting and writing local news for the *Indianapolis Star*, but for me retirement was a new and untraveled road. I did spadework for a possible consulting business on writing and editing. And I proposed and was hired for a new part-time summer job "mentoring" interns at Indiana newspapers for the Hoosier State Press Association. I had a heart-warming farewell party *cum* family reunion at the college, and journalism colleagues also put together their own farewell—each reading one of my poems. What great people! Karen and I then got comfortably through the summer, visiting newspapers together for the mentoring project. The house went to hell, but then it always had— that was why Janey, the cleaning whiz, came in every two weeks.

In August, we were to go to our son Mike's wedding in Kentucky, but three days before the ceremony, the mother of Amanda, the bride-to-be, died unexpectedly. The wedding was postponed, and we went to a funeral instead. Then on the way back from the cemetery, Amanda decided, after consultations, that she still wanted to marry Mike that day. So we had an evening wedding at the couple's house, thus ending on a joyous note a day that had begun in deep sorrow. Three days later, Karen and I flew to Vancouver for the wedding of Rick Hamilton and Jen Walters, the Canadian student described in Chapter 22. Then we vacationed in the Okanagan Valley of British Columbia before going to Port Townsend, Wash., to see another old friend, the poet Mike O'Connor, and do a workshop for *Vigilance*, an alternative newspaper there.

When we got home, the pear tree at the bottom of the garden had gone crazy. There was too much fruit for jam, so I decided to turn the crop into pear wine; an elderberry wine debacle of childhood was remote enough now to ignore. From Scotland, Edwin Wakeling, Ann's husband, was casual—just throw in yeast, sugar, and a handful of oatmeal, he said. Rick Hamilton, a partner in a Vancouver microbrewery, counseled a scientific approach with strict sanitation. I split the difference, and the seven gallons of pear wine turned out fine, as did a later two gallons of persimmon wine and some peach brandy.

I have now adopted the philosophy of William Hart, the hero of John Moore's *The Blue Field.* Before old William grew too stiff to totter down to the pub, he began making wine, on the sensible plan that supply should always exceed demand and that he would live to be 100 and would tend to drink more as he got older. Retirement should be happy around our house, whether Karen and I remember much of it or not. Beside the pear tree, under a willow, we put a bench, for which I wrote a poem for visitors:

> *We've put it under the willow*
> *where you can see out*
> *without being seen.*
> *It's like peering through*
> *a beaded curtain or*
> *in the attic a little window*
> *only you know is there.*
> *Be very quiet, listen,*
> *you can hear a pear ripening*
> *next door. A rabbit*
> *lopes toward you but stops*
> *to nibble violets. Even the sun*
> *thinks you're somewhere else.*

Our California friend, Marvin Sosna, whose newspaper my students had once voted the nation's best small-town one, wrote encouragingly from deeper in a very active retirement: "Enjoy the journey, find hope and excitement, expect worry and aches, open your arms and embrace the freedom you have chosen." In the end, it took about a year to make the retirement transition, during which I wrote *Under the Heaven Tree*, the childhood half of these memoirs.

So have Karen and I solved all the problems? Of course not. There is only one solution to the ache of existence; "If you had a limitless life it would be a real problem for you," the Zen master Shunryu Suzuki said. Recently, a small house fire, quickly extinguished, has reminded us of life's fragility and its potential for tragic endings—and also of the compassion and care of neighbors and friends.

Meanwhile, there is a garden to be planted this spring, and more pear wine to be made next fall. A trip is laid on in August to Karen's ancestral home in Denmark and a return to Inverness in Scotland. Ann Wakeling is going to St. Kilda again this summer, and we'll get her account firsthand. As this is written, a 30-year collection of poetry, *The Landscape Deeper In*, is at the publisher's, and a month from now I'll be getting to know the 10 students selected for this summer's internships at newspapers around Indiana.

Many years ago, driving in the fruit and melon country south of Vincennes, I passed an old man planting peach trees. His name was Ernie Pahmeier, and since he was nearly 90, he was planting an orchard from which he would probably never eat a peach. But Ernie wasn't thinking about that or making some statement about immortality. He had been planting orchards all his life and saw no reason to stop now.

In writing these memoirs, I've thought a lot about the future, especially that of our two granddaughters. Rebecca, 9, is the daughter of David and his wife Connie. Amber, 17, is the daughter of our son Mike's wife, Amanda, and has kindly agreed to be a granddaughter. We doubled our wealth overnight. Rebecca is the genetic descendant of the cloud of ancestors I wrote about in *Under the Heaven Tree*, but we imagine them all as happily adopting Amber. Wouldn't Kate, my grandmother, be delighted with both of them, and my parents, Eve and Jack, and Karen's parents, Fritz and Mary? And Amber comes from the old home ground of Kentucky and may even be a shirt-tail cousin, as indeed everybody is.

The idea of home ground occurs often in these memoirs, but all of us create it for ourselves. Franklin belongs to the past and the worlds of other people; I returned to it only by accident. Amber and Rebecca will each make her own world, as will some other storyteller 100 years hence. Rebecca will have a bit of the Virginia seacoast in hers, and the Kentucky hills will surely figure in Amber's. And for that distant storyteller, home ground may include the moon and stars.

But there will be a home, for as the poet Basho wrote: "Life is a journey, and the journey itself is home."

— Franklin, Indiana
March 14, 2005

Photo by Brad Bliss, Hornell, N.Y., 1965

ACKNOWLEDGMENTS

So many people helped in large and small ways with this book that there's no way to thank them all adequately. My biggest debt is to Karen, who encouraged this sequel and was its able first reader. She and our sons were also good-humored about my take on our lives together. Karl, in particular, gave special help in his capacity as a librarian and researcher.

Two friends, Mike O'Connor and Susanna Rich, both fine poets and expert writers generally, gave invaluable advice. I have been amazingly blessed in having two of what the Chinese call *chih-yin*—readers who understand my heart.

I am especially grateful to Gyanne Smith for her cover painting. She is the wife of an Army friend, Charlie Smith, and we were all together in Würzburg those many years ago. With us were Max Nichols and Bill Manly, who helped refresh my memory of those days. Cover preparation and typography were again in the capable hands of Lindsay Hadley.

Jen Walters Hamilton of Vancouver, B.C., has my deep gratitude for allowing use of material from her letters and her life. I'm also pleased to be able to use an excerpt from the wedding poem written for her and her husband, Rick Hamilton.

To the correspondents mentioned in Chapter 16, what a lot of fun we've had! Besides others already named, here or earlier in the text, I think with special affection of Marvin Sosna, Bill Manly, Judy Robbins, France Yu, Jerry Reddan, Linda Yew, Tammy Peng, Tove Eivindsen, and Grace Fan, an avatar of the Fabulous Girl and my tutor in Chinese over several years. There are more who are not regular correspondents but whom it is a delight to hear from.

To try to single out all the students who have influenced this book would inevitably leave many out, but I can hardly *not* mention the Brat Pack—Steve Polston, Mary Beth Wakefield, and Denny Hager—or Sarah LeBarron Simmons, Andy Stoner, Connie Swaim, and Rachel Sheeley, who allowed me to quote her immortal opening to the world's worst novel. And Sheri Herrin, whose horse was sick. I also owe a special debt to many at Franklin College, who helped me do things I wanted to do, sometimes with rather thin academic justification. And to the late Harvey C. Jacobs, a fine writer and lifelong influence, and Cliff Cain, with whom I have roamed the world. And Arliene Britt, one of several super-secretaries I've had; Page 166 indicates what they had to put up with. And finally I mention with sadness a friend and co-worker in Taipei, Jessica Chen, gone much too soon.

In the pursuit of elusive data, I had help from several friends and former faculty colleagues, among them Jerry Miller, Jayne Marek, and Ron Schuetz. Ron heads a Franklin College Library staff that has been unfailingly helpful. Also at the college, Cody Crocker, Mark Lecher, and Dennis Cripe supplied crucial computer advice and help. Susie Fleck, a superb photographer and teacher, is largely responsible for my photos not being worse than they are. I am grateful to Brad Bliss, former photographer at the Hornell *Evening Tribune,* for his photos from that time. Karen and I, two fairly penniless newlyweds, also want to thank David W. Jackson of Vincennes, Indiana, who took our wedding pictures as a gift. (Still no money, Dave, but you finally get a credit line.)

A fine woodworker, Emmett Newkirk, assisted with a technical point, as did Amy McKune, collections manager of the Eiteljorg Museum in Indianapolis. Vicco and Lilo von Stralendorff helped me check German spellings.

Some of those who perhaps deserve the most thanks cannot be credited, even though your lives touched mine and helped make it and these memoirs what they are. You are the friends, the teachers, the newspaper and college colleagues, the casual acquaintances. You are the unknown girl whose red skirt flickered around a corner for an instant and was gone, never to be forgotten. Thank you, whoever and wherever you are.

* * *

Bill Manly, mentioned often in these pages, died on July 9, 2005, after an illness—a good friend, a kind heart, and a brave man.

SELECTED INDEX OF NAMES

Spaceship #1 by Colin Bridges